THE TREASURES OF
TIFFANY

A special exhibition presented by the Chicago Tribune at the Museum of Science and Industry in Chicago from the collection of the Charles Hosmer Morse Foundation

by Hugh F. McKean
President, Charles Hosmer Morse Foundation

June 10-November 14, 1982,

Published by Chicago Review Press, Chicago

MUSEUM OF SCIENCE & INDUSTRY·CHICAGO

Table of Contents

Book design by Joseph M. Essex

Cover: Detail from "Autumn" from The Four Seasons, window designed by Tiffany in 1900.

Photographs on pages 8, 12, 15, 17, 26, 30, 34, 40, 52 and 58 are from The "Lost" Treasures of Louis Comfort Tiffany *© 1980 by Hugh F. McKean. Reproduced by permission of Doubleday & Company, Inc.*

Black-and-white photographs of Laurelton Hall from the Tiffany Studios.

All other photographs by permission of the Charles Hosmer Morse Foudnation.

Published by Chicago Review Press, 213 West Institute Place, Chicago, Illinois 60610

Library of Congress Number 82-4590

Foreword

Victor J. Danilov
President and Director
Museum of Science and
Industry Chicago

The beautiful stained glass windows, lamps, vases, and other artistic creations of Louis Comfort Tiffany (1848-1933) have been both highly prized and virtually ignored. At the turn of the century, Tiffany was being hailed the leading American exponent of the Art Nouveau style. His colorful works of glass were eagerly sought for homes, churches, offices, and museums.

In the years that followed, "Tiffany glass" gradually fell out of favor. It was considered to be exceedingly ornate and theatrical in nature. The art world also looked down upon Tiffany's factory-produced art works.

Then came a resurgence of interest as Tiffany was rediscovered. He was praised for his innovative techniques, brilliant colors, imaginative designs, unusual shapes, and range of talents.

Today, Louis Comfort Tiffany is regarded as a major figure in the history of glass and manufactured art. His multilayered stained glass windows, dragonfly and peony lamps, floriform vases, iridescent mosaics, and other works have become treasured possessions.

Tiffany turned his back on his father's jewelry business and forsook a promising career as a painter to become a creator of spectacular works of glass, bronze, ceramics, copper, enamel, and other materials. Many of the early products were made and signed by Tiffany. As the demand became greater, he hired craftsmen to execute his designs under his personal direction. An important stepping stone in Tiffany's career was the design and production of a Chapel for the 1892 World's Columbian Exposition in Chicago. It was one of the highlights of the world's fair and opened new avenues for the art glass entrepeneur. The Tiffany materials come from the collection of the Charles Hosmer Morse Foundation, which operates the Morse Gallery of Art in Winter Park, Florida. It is the greatest collection of Tiffany works in the world, containing some 4,000 pieces. The Tiffany materials were gathered by Hugh F. and Jeannette McKean. They salvaged the remains from a fire that swept Laurelton Hall, Tiffany's country estate on Long Island, and through the years collected other works from many different sources.

In 1930, Mr. McKean spent two months painting landscapes and living at Laurelton Hall under the auspices of the Louis Comfort Tiffany Foundation, founded by Tiffany to bring young artists under the spell of Laurelton Hall and his collections. Mrs. McKean is the former Jeannette Genius of Chicago. She is a granddaughter of the late Charles Hosmer Morse, once president of the Fairbanks Morse Company.

We thank the Morse Foundation and Mr. and Mrs. McKean for making it possible to exhibit a portion of their Tiffany collection, and the Chicago Tribune *for presenting the showing in cooperation with the Morse Foundation and the Museum of Science and Industry.*

Prologue: How the Collection Began

Living Room at Laurelton Hall, "The Bathers" Window in Background

*L*ouis Tiffany as a person was an influence in my life long before I owned any Tiffany glass. In the spring of 1930, I graduated from college. During September and October of that fall, I lived and worked at Laurelton Hall, the summer place Tiffany had built on 580 acres of woodlands and gardens overlooking Cold Spring Harbor on Long Island's North Shore. I was one of fifteen fortunate young people who had received a fellowship from the Louis Comfort Tiffany Foundation.

Tiffany had created his Foundation in 1918 — he was seventy at the time — in order to carry out his "dearest wish," that of helping young people headed for a career in the arts. He endowed the Foundation with $1,500,000.00 and gave it Laurelton Hall, which housed his finest leaded windows, his extensive collections of Oriental art, ancient glass, and American Indian Art. He designed and built Laurelton Hall in 1903-1904 at a cost of $214,079.64. He also built the small museum standing near the house, which he filled with paintings by himself and by some of his contemporaries.

Tiffany's plan was characteristically imaginative. A jury would invite promising painters, sculptors, designers, jewelers, photographers, and printmakers to spend periods of two months living and working at Laurelton Hall as his guests. There would be no instruction. He was confident the beauty of the place, with its terraces, gardens, and vast art collections, would inspire his proteges to find a beauty of their own.

Laurelton Hall ran three hundred feet along high ground overlooking the harbor. Its thirty or more rooms included a library, a Chinese room, and a smoking room. A three-storied court capped with a blue glass dome held a pipe organ in its upper floors. A fountain on the ground floor was fed by a stream which rose from the neck of a slender vase, flowed down its sides into a basin, and continued on through a marble trough to fountains and terraces beyond. Light colors predominated in the court's painted woodwork, velvet cushions, and mosaic floors; flowers and tropical plants were everywhere. The estate had a breathtaking, fresh kind of beauty.

Tiffany himself was eighty-two when I was at Laurelton Hall in 1930. After dazzling the late Victorians with the brilliance of his creations, he had fallen out of fashion. In the 1920s, his work was thrown out with the trash and he was ridiculed by many critics. This kind of rejection can brew bitterness, but Mr. Tiffany's mind was on other things. His blue eyes twinkled with kindness. He was gracious, friendly, reserved, and displayed the self-confidence and dignity of those who accomplish their goals and are secure in their convictions. He was happy showing others how beauty can become part of everyday life. I left Laurelton Hall with great admiration for him and all he represented.

My wife Jeannette as a young woman had her own introduction to Tiffany. Her grandfather Charles Hosmer Morse's granite house on Chicago's Greenwood Avenue in Kenwood was designed by Bell and Swift in the creative spirit of Louis Sullivan. Mr. Morse's residence in Florida was a Craftsman house. Both contained handsome pieces of Tiffany's Favrile glass. Tiffany was an early and lasting influence.

Jeannette and I never decided to collect anything, but in 1953, when I was serving as Director of Rollins' Morse Gallery of Art and she was Director of Exhibitions, she began to plan for an exhibition of Tiffany glass.

Since her family pieces were not enough to make a show, we began to search the second-hand shops on New York's Third Avenue. This was a tedious process and we asked the Metropolitan Museum of Art in New York and the Smithsonian Institution in Washington for loans from their collections. The Metropolitan was especially gracious. It not only agreed to lend some pieces, but offered them as a gift explaining they were not needed. The Smithsonian lent many things, but wanted them back.

Our exhibition from February 21 to March 31, 1955, was the first Tiffany Exhibition in modern times and it was beautifully reviewed by *the* New York Times.

Meanwhile, Laurelton Hall was in trouble. Tiffany had died in 1933. The depression had reduced the Foundation's income. Laurelton Hall was drafty, cold in winter, out of fashion in all seasons, costly to maintain, and in the view of the directors of the Tiffany Foundation (and nearly everyone else), a big white elephant. In 1949, they sold the structure and four acres of land for $10,000 (it once had been valued in the millions). Subsequent owners could find no use for it, and in 1957 "mysterious" fires roared through the building. Firefighters from the nearby towns worked without rest for three long days (neighbors brought food and drink), but it was hopeless. Thoughtful persons had removed some of the windows, lamps, and furniture. However, the place was gutted by flames.

Shortly after the fire, Comfort Gilder, one of Tiffany's twin daughters, wrote suggesting that we try to save three windows she understood had not been destroyed. On a visit to the ruins, we found windows stacked in the Chapel, and the Chapel open and abandoned. The "Daffodil Terrace" and "Loggia" were largely intact; the dining room furniture was scattered over the grounds; and bulldozers were waiting to clear it all away. At Jeannette's suggestion, we purchased all that was left — everything.

We now owned an assortment of enormous columns, weather-beaten furniture, building fragments, and stacks of leaded windows, some of which weighed hundreds of pounds. We also had twisted pieces of God only knew what. No museum was interested in our "collection," and no dealer would have taken it on any terms. We did the only thing possible, we shipped it all to Florida. That is how our collection began.

8.

View of Fountain Court, showing Vase at Center

Vase from Fountain Court at Laurelton Hall (#1)

*L*aurelton Hall, built in 1903-1904, was influenced by Art Nouveau, but it also had unique characteristics. The many-roomed stuccoed mansion followed no known pattern, reflected a strong Oriental influence, and was graced with an elegant simplicity. Its light colors gave it a weightless quality; glass walls had the effect of making the terraces, gardens, and views of the harbor an integral part of the house itself. Marble, glass, concrete, lead, and wood were combined in strange and wonderful ways. It was "new art," different from the stylistic revivals of the Victorians.

Laurelton Hall reflected the search for new art forms, but it had none of the swinging lines and backlash curves so often associated with European Art Nouveau.

The vase-fountain from the Fountain Court, for example, has the simple lines of a drop of water. It is clear glass with a hole in the bottom to admit the water that flowed gently down its sides into a surrounding basin and then through a marble trough to the terraces beyond. Colored lights hidden underneath changed its color slowly from green to blue to violet. (The golden tones the vase now has are due to mineral deposits from the water.)

The "Daffodil Terrace" was named for the yellow glass flowers set in the concrete capitals topping its marble columns. (These capitals are an early use of precast concrete.) The ceiling of the terrace was made of stenciled wood and ceramic tiles. The blue glass screen with a pattern of pear tree leaves was designed by Tiffany for an opening he left in the terrace roof so an old pear tree could live on undisturbed by the addition of the terrace.

While all these fragments are from the ruins, they may not have been part of the building itself. The heavy lead downspout set with glass jewels, for example, may be from elsewhere. All that is known for certain is that it was found in the debris of Laurelton Hall.

The strange, badly damaged old door is of particular interest. It was once decorated with part of Tiffany's collection of Japanese sword guards, which numbered in the thousands. This fragment bears the prints or "ghosts" of many of the sword guards, which have since disappeared. The villian who pried them off overlooked one, which may be the sole survivor of Tiffany's great collection.

Laurelton Hall was Louis Tiffany's most lavish creation, but he did not draw the plans himself. They were the work of Robert L. Pryor, a brilliant young draftsman employed by the Tiffany Studios. Pryor, who had no formal training as an architect, left the Tiffany Studios in 1904 to establish a decorating firm of his own, and not long after that he devoted all his time to the practice of architecture.

In a conversation with Dorothy Burlingham, Tiffany's youngest daughter, long before I knew about Pryor, I remarked that her father surely had someone else make the working drawings for Laurelton Hall. Her reply was: "If someone else made those drawings it was someone who would do exactly what Papa wanted." She was absolutely right.

Fragments

1. *Vase from Fountain Court. Designed by Louis C. Tiffany, 1902-1904. Ht. 49 in.*

2. *Capitals from Daffodil Terrace; designed by Louis C. Tiffany after 1904. Cement set with Favrile glass blossoms and stems. Ht. 22¼ in.*

3. *Two Pear Tree panels from opening in Daffodil Terrace; designed by Louis C. Tiffany after 1904. Six-inch squares of decorated iridescent Favrile glass mounted on wood. Ht. 25¼ in.*

4. *Cast lead architectural element in cobra design with glass-jewel inserts. 8 x 29 in.*

5. *Gilded cast lead fragment with glass-jewel inserts. 14 x 24 in.*

6. *Cast lead architectural fragment with molded Favrile glass inserts. Possibly a down spout. Ht. 6 in.*

7. *Copper fragment set with molded green Favrile glass jewels. Ht. 4½ in.*

8. *Pale green molded glass hanging light fixture. Ht. 4 in.*

9. *Pale green molded glass ornament, en suite with 5. Ht. 9 in.*

10. *Ceramic tile from ceiling in Daffodil Terrace. 14 x 14 in.*

11. *Yellow Favrile glass tile fragment from Daffodil Terrace. Ht. 6 in.*

12. *Yellow Favrile glass tile fragment from Daffodil Terrace, en suite with 8.*

13. *Blown-glass dome from Fountain Court; signed L.C.T. Dia. 6½ in.*

14. *Favrile glass tile similar to those used in Loggia; glass fragments embedded in surface. 4 x 4 in.*

15. *Blown glass ceiling light shade from Fountain Court; signed L. C. Tiffany — Favrilite-Glass. Dia. 6 in.*

16. *Molded iridescent blue glass tile from Loggia. 4 x 4 in.*

17. *White glazed brick tile from dining-room fireplace. Signed TIFFANY, with N reversed (И) L. 12 in.*

18. *Hand-stenciled wood panel from ceiling in Daffodil Terrace L 12 in.*

19. *Ornamental plaque; ca. 1900. Painted plaster inset with glass; 24 x 23 in. Found in the ruins of Laurelton Hall.*

20. *Fragments of Leaded glass window. Found in the ruins of Laurelton Hall*

21. *Working drawings for Laurelton Hall. The overall design was by Louis Comfort Tiffany. The drawings were by Robert L. Pryor an employee of Tiffany Studios.*

The Alan Dunn Watercolors

Alan Dunn, the famous cartoonist whose drawings brightened the New Yorker *for decades, was a Tiffany Fellow. The watercolors in this exhibit were made by Dunn during the times he spent at Laurelton Hall.*

22. *View of Daffodil Terrace, ca. 1925.*

23. *Loggia of Laurelton Hall, ca. 1925.*

24. *Loggia of Laurelton Hall, ca. 1925.*

The Windows: Should One Use the Brush?

Jesus Blessing St. John. From the World's Columbian Exposition Chapel, 1892 (#43)

*M*aking leaded windows was Tiffany's first venture into an art form other than painting. He began making windows because glass always had fascinated him, and because he realized that windows could reach people who had no interest in pictures.

Tiffany's first windows, made in the mid-1870s, were simple decorative screens of colored glass. Then came those with human figures, and with them a problem. Should he use enamels (powdered colored glass painted on clear glass with a brush and then fired) to get natural effects, or should he listen to his aesthetic conscience and construct the entire window, figures and all, with pieces of untreated glass?

For parts other than faces and hands, Tiffany had the answer — glass that suggested pictorial effects. He invented every kind of glass he could imagine. Some was wrinkled and folded before it cooled so it would look like the drapery itself (drapery glass). He had threads of dark glass embedded in lighter colored glass to suggest twigs. The surface of some glass was rippled to suggest water. He made sky glass and sunset glass. Several different colors were combined in the same sheet to suggest marble. It was new and beautiful. No one had ever seen anything like it before.

Eventually, the Tiffany Studios had thousands of sheets of different kinds and colors of glass, all about three feet long, and all color coded and stored so the right glass could be found to suggest any effect Tiffany wanted. The one exception was flesh tones. In the "Entombment" window, the figures were executed in enamels. Eventually, as in "Creation" and "Geology" from "The Tree of Life," he succeeded in getting flesh tones in the glass itself, but the brush was still used for details and shading.

13.

"Creation" from The Tree of Life Window, 1930 (#30)

"Feeding the Flamingoes," which Tiffany designed for the World's Columbian Exposition, is a triumph of glassmaking. While the face and arms are enamel, the bowl with the swirling goldfish is untreated glass. The jet of water shooting up in the fountain is a streak of clear glass pulled through the dark glass with a hook. All the rest is a mosaic of pieces of glass so cleverly selected and fitted together that they suggest long-legged birds standing beside a fountain in a Roman villa.

The maiden's feet are covered by her robes. Tiffany disliked using the brush because it meant he could not rely on his medium to get the effects he wanted, and toes would have meant more enameling. He was proud of "Summer" and "Autumn," from the "Four Seasons," because they were untouched with a brush.

This exhibition contains many windows Tiffany designed himself. They are not well-known because most of them remained in his own collection and the public has had few opportunities to see them.

25. Feeding the Flamingoes. *Leaded window from painting by Louis C. Tiffany, c 1892. Signed* Tiffany Glass & Dec. Co., 333-334 4th Ave., N.Y. *Made for the World's Columbian Exposition, Chicago, 1893. Ht. 62 in.*

26. Grape Arbor Window. *Leaded glass window depicting clusters of grapes, vines and leaves pendant from an arbor against a background of sky. From a private residence in Pennsylvania. Unsigned. Length 87 in.*

27. The Scholar. *Leaded window depicting a cloistered monk working on an illuminated manuscript. Made by Tiffany Glass and Decorating Company, c. 1892, for the World's Columbian Exposition but signed at a later date* Tiffany Studios New York. *Ht. 29 in.*

28. Pumpkin and Beets. *Leaded window designed by Louis C. Tiffany in the Impressionist style seen in his c. 1900 painting* Sow with Piglets: *1900-5, unsigned. Ht. 47 in.*

29. Snowball. *Leaded transom depicting snowballs and wisteria, designed by Louis C. Tiffany for Laurelton Hall c. 1904; unsigned. Ht. 27 in.*

30. Creation, *from* The Tree of Life *window. Leaded circular panel of multi-colored and enameled glass showing Adam and Eve in the Garden of Eden (Eve is holding an apple); one of six leaded panels (the others depicting Science, Geology, Entombment, Astronomy, and Religion) which make up the last leaded window Tiffany designed and made; 1930, unsigned. Dia. 23 in.*

31. Geology, *from* The Tree of Life *window. Leaded circular panel portraying a venerable figure holding a rock and explaining it to an attentive group; 1930, unsigned. Dia. 23 in.*

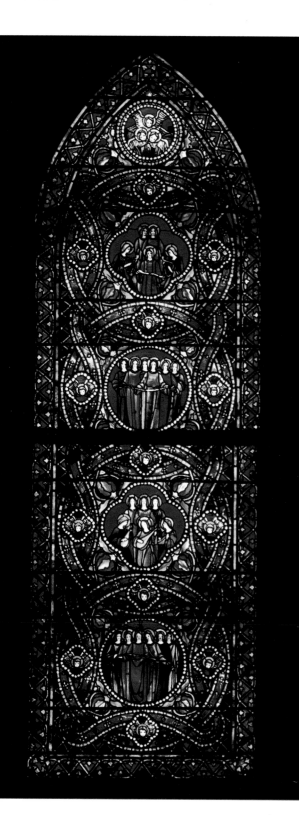

The Scholar Window. Designed for
the World's Columbian Exposition,
1892 (#27)

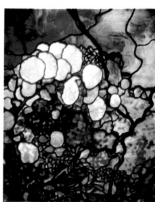

Snowball Window. Designed for
Laurelton Hall, c. 1904 (#29)

Medallion Window. Designed for
the World's Columbian Exposition
Chapel, 1892 (#46)

Entombment Window. Made for the World's Columbian Exposition Chapel, 1892 (#42)

32. Pebble. *Leaded window from the Joseph Briggs residence (Briggs was Tiffany's business manager); two medallions composed of quartz pebbles and clear glass chips in a pattern suggesting flower forms, vertically positioned in a panel of mottled amber glass topped by a Gothic arch and surrounded by a frame of quartz pebbles, square red "jewels," and amber glass. Made by Tiffany Studios after 1902; unsigned. Ht. 61 in.*

33. Symbolic window. *Leaded window containing abstract Art Nouveau design on greenish-yellow textured ground, framed by translucent opalescent-white tiles; 1892-1900. Made by Tiffany Glass and Decorating Company and displayed for years in the Tiffany Studios showrooms; unsigned. 31 c 43¼ in.*

34. Magnolia. *Three of seven leaded window panels designed by Louis C. Tiffany for the Tiffany mansion at 72nd Street and Madison Avenue, New York City. c. 1885; unsigned. Ht. 48 in.*

35. Eggplant. *Leaded transom possibly from the George Kemp residence in New York City, which was decorated by Louis C. Tiffany in 1879; leaves and highly decorative eggplants on a trellis; unsigned. Leaded eggplant stems provide support for glass sections. Ht. 32 in.*

36. Summer. *Leaded window once part of the large* Four Seasons *window designed by Louis C. Tiffany and shown at the 1900 Paris* Exposition Universelle; *this section pictures foliage and poppies against a landscape background. Ht. 39 in.*

37. Autumn *from* Four Seasons. *This section depicts an array of fruit and vegetables suggesting harvest abundance. Ht. 39 in.*

38. Wisteria. *Leaded transom showing dense clusters of wisteria blossoms and leaves pendent from a trellis; designed by Louis C. Tiffany for the dining room at Laurelton Hall c. 1910; unsigned 36 x 47 in.*

39. *Four leaded door panels made for the Heckscher residence, depicting graceful vines bearing blossoms, fruit, and vegetables against trellis background; c 1905. Tiffany Studios; unsigned. Ht. 122 in.*

40. Jeweled transom. *Once part of the border of Tiffany's* Adoration *window, this leaded transom is made up of small, brilliant pieces of varicolored glass combined to give a jeweled effect; 1900-1916, unsigned 8½ x 87 in.*

42. Entombment. *Leaded window depicting the entombment of Christ; made by Tiffany for the World's Columbian Exposition chapel c. 1892; unsigned. Tiffany used his father, jeweler Charles L. Tiffany, as model for the face of Joseph of Arimathea (shown supporting the body of Jesus). Ht. 104 in.*

43. Jesus Blessing St. John. *Leaded window designed by Louis C. Tiffany for the World's Columbian Exposition chapel, c. 1892. Tiffany Glass and Decorating Company; unsigned. Dia. 104 in.*

44. Lily. *Leaded window designed by Louis C. Tiffany for the World's Columbian Exposition chapel, as it was installed at Laurelton Hall c. 1916; unsigned. Originally figure of an angel occupied the central area of this window. Ht. 139 in.*

45. Christ, Ruler of the Universe. *Leaded window in form of a Greek cross, depicting Christ with orb and scepter surrounded by medallions containing New Testament scenes; designed by Louis C. Tiffany for the World's Columbian Exposition chapel, c. 1892. Tiffany Glass and Decorating Company; unsigned. Dia. 105 in.*

46. Medallion. *Lancet-form leaded window designed by Louis C. Tiffany in the Gothic mode of the thirteenth century; one small and four large medallions, vertically aligned, show angelic musicians, the whole in particularly glowing colors. Made for exhibition c. 1892 and unsigned. Ht. 146 in.*

Feeding the Flamingoes. Made for the World's Columbian Exposition, 1892 (#25)

Eggplant Window. Possibly from George Kemp residence in New York City, decorated by Tiffany 1879 (#35)

Tiffany: A Painter First

Sow With Piglets. C. 1900. Watercolor on paper (#67)

My Family at Somesville. Oil Painting on Canvas, 1888 (#64)

*L*ouis Tiffany began his art career as a painter and remained a painter all his life. As a sixteen-year-old, he won an award for "proficiency in drawing" from Eagleswood Military Academy. A book of sketches, made in 1865 on his first trip to Europe, is filled with delightful drawings and watercolors.

The extent of Tiffany's formal art training is not clear. He chose to study art rather than attend college, but "study" seems to have meant watching his teachers (George Inness and later Leon Bailly) paint. He seems to have leap-frogged the traditional routine of drawing from plaster casts and nude models, and he may be a good example of the artist "who never had a lesson in his life."

Even so, success came early to the young Tiffany. His canvasses were accepted in national shows before he was out of his teens. At twenty-three, he was elected an associate of the National Academy of Design and in his thirty-second year he was elected an Academician. Something else pleased Tiffany very much: he was financially successful as a painter. He was able to sell his pictures for as much as much as five hundred dollars when that sum would build a house.

Tiffany was too expansive in his interests, however, to limit himself to painting easel pictures. Along with William Morris, Henry van de Velde, Frank Brangwyn, and other concerned artists of the time, he wanted to put more art in daily life. And by art, he did not mean curlicues cut with a band saw or vases made by a machine.

Tiffany was intelligent and restless. He knew that many well-intentioned Americans were bored with the rows of pictures in museums. He was an alert businessman as well and liked to make money. He also knew there was money as well as satisfaction in the so-called decorative arts. Before he was finished, he had worked creatively in many diverse art forms.

Even so, he remained a dedicated painter all his long life. His early pictures contain detailed images made with careful touches of a sable hair brush held by a hand resting on a mahlstick. In the 1880s, he is using a bristle brush loaded with pigment. "Peonies and Iris," painted in 1915, is Impressionism, dashing brush strokes, broken colors, and all. It records the light reflected from the flowers, not the surfaces of the flowers.

The camera, which appeared in the first half of the 19th century, caused considerable indigestion in art circles. Some French academicians called on the government to ban the device which they considered unfair competition. Others used photographs with the shades drawn. A few simply gave up. Tiffany, never at odds with the technological advances of his own times, welcomed photography as a new art form, tried his hand at it, and used photographs as an aid in his painting.

Two versions of "My Family at Somesville" survive, a small sketch dashed off in a few minutes and a completed picture with the clarity and precision of a photograph. A third version must have been a photograph taken just after he made the color sketch.

Tiffany thought of himself as a colorist and an innovator until the Armory Show held in New York in 1913. In that exhibition the French Abstract Expressionsists shook America out of its complacency with patterns in strong colors which bore some resemblance to real objects, but not very much. Tiffany glared at the brilliant and provocative pictures and blew his stack. To him pure colors were glorious in glass but not in paintings. He believed the paintbrush should record what the eye sees, not concoct things that "hurt" the eye. In other art forms, Tiffany loved to break rules. But as a painter, he was a traditionalist: a good *traditionalist, that is.*

Watercolor designs

47. *Study for a triptych leaded glass window. Watercolor and tempera on paper. Scale 1 in. to 1 ft. Total image: ht. 4⅜ x width 6¾ in.*

48. *Study for a leaded glass window. Watercolor and pencil on paper. Scale: 1 in. to 1 ft. Total image: ht. 5½ x width 9½ in.*

49. *Study for a mausoleum leaded glass window. Watercolor and pencil on paper. Scale: 2 in. x 1 ft. Total image: ht. 10⅜ x width 4¾ in.*

50. *Study for a wall light. Watercolor on paper. Total image: ht. 13½ x width 10¼ in.*

51. *Study for a Newel lamp. Watercolor on paper. Total image: ht. 13½ x width 10¼.*

52. The Art Work of Louis Comfort Tiffany. *1914 Cover designed by Louis C. Tiffany and anonymously written by Charles de Kay at Tiffany's request, published by Doubleday, Page and Co. Fly leaf inscribed: "No 1 — to Mr. and Mrs. Charles L. Tiffany, My dear son and daughter, Merry Xmas 1914."*

53. *Same as above, no inscription. Unbound and was Louis Comfort Tiffany's personal copy.*

54. *On the Hudson River at Dobbs Ferry, ca. 1880. Oil on canvas; 12½ x 27½ in. Signed:* Louis C. Tiffany. *This particular painting demonstrates the strong influence of his teacher, George Inness.*

55. *Figure study of an Arab, ca. 1875. Watercolor on paper; 14 x 7½ in., unsigned. One of a number of figural and costume studies done by Tiffany in the 1870s while in North Africa.*

56. *Figure study of an Arab, ca. 1875. Oil on canvas; 9¼ x 7½ in. Pencil inscription on mat:* Painted by Louis C. Tiffany.

57. *Figure study of an Arab, ca. 1875. Oil on canvas; 10 x 7½ in. Pencil inscription on mat:* Painted by Louis C. Tiffany.

58. *Figure study of an Arab musician, ca. 1875. Water color on paper; 9½ x 7½ in. Unsigned.*

59. Fruit vendors under the sea wall at Nassau, *1872. Oil on canvas; 8½ x 10½ in.; signed lower left:* L. Tiffany. *Frame designed by Louis C. Tiffany.*

60. European Merchant's House, *1877. Watercolor on paper; 11½ x 18½ in. Signed lower right:* Louis C. Tiffany.

61. Old Mill at Frieburg, *1877. Watercolor on paper; 13½ x 19½ in. Signed lower right:* Louis C. Tiffany.

62. Study of Woman at Market, *undated. Oil on wood panel; 6¾ x 5½ in. Unsigned.*

63. My Family at Somesville, *ca. 1888. Oil study on wood panel for larger painting; 5¼ x 8¼ in. Unsigned.*

64. My Family at Somesville, *1888. Oil on canvas; 24 x 36 in. Unsigned. From the small oil sketch, this scene depicts Tiffany's wife, children and their nanny enjoying the fields near Somesville, Maine.*

65. Night in a Tropical Garden, *ca. 1890. Oil on canvas; 23 x 28 in. Signed lower right:* Louis C. Tiffany. *This scene is compiled of architectural elements from the 7th floor studio in the 72nd Street mansion and Louis Tiffany's keen imagination.*

66. Spring, *ca. 1898. Oil on canvas; 58½ x 94' in. Signed lower left:* Louis C. Tiffany. *Lacking academic training, Tiffany's figural allegory is rather awkward. However, his ability to interpret nature was excellent, both on canvas or in glass.*

67. Sow with Piglets, *ca. 1900. Watercolor on paper, 19 x 24¾ in. Signed lower right:* Louis C. Tiffany. *Frame designed by Louis C. Tiffany.*

68. Palm Trees at Karnac, *dated 1908. Watercolor on paper; 26¾ x 19¾ in. Inscribed lower left:* Karnac Feb 08, *signed lower right:* LCT. *One of the studies painted on Tiffany's 1908 trip up the Nile.*

69. Yellowstone Canyon, *dated 1917. Watercolor on paper; 17¾ x 11¾ in. Signed lower left:* Louis C. Tiffany. *Tiffany, who traveled in a private railroad car, painted this on one of his trips out west.*

70. *Certificate for profiency in drawing. Awarded to Louis C. Tiffany in 1864.*

Tiffany's Contemporaries:
Their Work Compared with Tiffany's

A careful comparison of Tiffany's work with that of his contemporaries reveals both his conformity with the decorative style of his day and his departures from it. The organic line and the love of nature run through all the pieces, as do the emphasis on the "handmade" and the joy in materials. The painted decorations on the other art pottery call attention to the absence of pictures on Tiffany's. Gallé's glass, which Tiffany repeatedly acknowledged as an influence on his own, underscores the simplicity in most of Tiffany's.

The wooden clock covered with a thin sheet of metal set with glass jewels and signed "Alf. Daguet" was made for S. Bing's Paris shop, "Le Salon de L'Art Nouveau" (This shop gave the Turn-of-the-Century Movement its most generally accepted name.) It was Bing who "discovered" Tiffany in the World's Columbian Exposition and who introduced his windows and glass to Europe. The clock has a handmade look; it is set with glass jewels; the design derives from natural forms; but it is more whimsical and less substantial than similar pieces by Tiffany.

After looking at the work of Tiffany's contemporaries, one can see more easily that, in spite of their diversity, all the things that came from Tiffany's shops and furnaces have a common look, whether they were designed by him or by designers on his staff.

A comparison also will call attention to the absence in Tiffany's work of the sinuous lady who adds such charm to a lot of Art Nouveau. This captivating individual is different from the noble woman with the vacant stare who appears so often in classic art: the Statue of Liberty being a magnificent example. The Art Nouveau woman is young, capricious, and singularly free of lofty thoughts. Her interests are parties, fun, and, above all, men.

Tiffany, a man of the world, traveled in his private railroad car, drank the finest wines, and crossed the ocean on the most luxurious liners, but his character was laced with the puritan ethics of his New England ancestors. The women in his windows usually are enveloped in drapery glass, but even when they wear nothing at all (as in "The Bathers," which burned with Laurelton Hall), they are as pure as Pear's transparent soap.

Contemporaries' Work

71. *Bowl. Incurved bucket form on low cylindrical foot; orange, brown, and pale-brown glass acid-etched in leaf-and-flower motif. Ht. 6 in. Marked* Gallé *with star.*

72. *Vase. Tall cylindrical neck on low spherical body: in amber-brown glass etched and enameled in multicolored raised floral motif. Ht. 14½ in. Marked* Cristallerie Emile Gallé A Nancy Modèle et Décor Déposés, *with oak leaves.*

73. *Vase. Cylindrical form with three-lobed rim; dark-green glass decorated in marquetry technique with purple iris blossom, pale-green and cream-color stems and leaves. Ht. 21 in. Marked* Gallé.

74. *Lamp. Flower-form in deep and pale shades of pink darkening to carnelian on standard; acid etched in botanical detail. Ht. 18½ in. Marked* Gallé.

75. *Compote. Pottery incurved conical form with two opposing pairs of stem-like handles, on square pedestal base; molded leaf decoration; golden-bronze and reddish-purple glaze over all. Ht. 10 in.* Amphora-Austria *mark.*

76. *Statuette. Pottery figure of woman in billowing bronze-toned gown rising from pale ochre water and resting her arms on green lily pads on either side; another woman's face is visible in the water at her feet. Ht. 21 in.* Amphora-Austria *mark.*

77. *Vase. Four-sided curvilinear form of thin white porcelain decorated with blue, purple, yellow, and red blossoms and green, blue, and gray foliage. Ht. 6½ in.* Rosenburg den Haag *mark.*

78. *Ewer. Four-sided baluster form of thin white porcelain with conical spout and drawn handle extending from body to neck; decorated with yellow blossoms, green leaves and birds. Ht. 8 in.* Rozenburg den Haag *mark.*

79. *Vase. Trumpet form in amber glass with bubble inclusions, resting in copper base formed of four vertical hand-tooled leaves; conical foot. Ht. 6 in. Glass marked* Steuben, *base marked* Roycroft *with R monogram.*

80. *Vase. Squat bulbous form in iridescent gold glass, with spool neck and flared circular rim; lower two-thirds cased in dark green with hooked decoration of iridescent gold. Ht. 4 in. Marked* Quezel.

81. *Vase. Inverted conical form in iridescent glass with spool neck and flared circular rim; wide dark-blue stripes with edges and background of variegated gold. Ht. 12 in. Marked* Durand V 20120-12.

82. *Vase. Trumpet form in iridescent gold glass cased in white; gold spool-shape base and conical foot; decorated with blue feather overlay edge in gold and random raised gold threading over all. Ht. 12¼ in. Marked* Durand V 20120-12.

83. *Fan Vase. Flattened conical shape in iridescent blue with creamy-tan decorative band of vines and leaves near top; baluster stem conical foot. Ht. 8½ in. Marked* Steuben Aurene 6297.

84. *Vase. Elongated bucket shape in pottery with molded forms of sea horses on sides, copper-tone glaze; resting in pot metal framework of ropes rising from rock-like base ornamented with an octopus with tiger's-eye cabochons for eyes, three moonstones, and two fresh-water pearls. Ht. 15½ in. Marked* M.L.S. *for Maria Longworth Storer, founder of the Rockwood Pottery.*

85. *Creamer. Irregular short vertical form in pottery with pouring spout and rectangular handle; purple-blue mottled exterior and brown interior glaze. Ht. 4 in. Marked* G.E. Ohr.

86. *Vase. Tall conical pottery form with metal rim, silver-metal-over-pottery base in octopus form; brown and ochre-gold glaze on body, decorated with seaweed motif. Ht. 18½ in.* Rockwood-Shirayamadani *mark.*

87. *Vase. Four-sided incurved bucket form in pottery with two opposing handles; stylized floral decoration, on deep-blue iridescent glaze. Ht. 6 in. Marked* Weller Sicard.

88. *Vase. Bulbous conical form in pottery with spool neck and flared circular rim; variegated brown to orange-brown exterior, orange interior glaze; pitcher-plant motif on exterior. Ht. 11½ in.* Rookwood-Valentien *mark.*

89. *Lamp base/Vase. Elongated incurved bucket form in pottery with green matte glaze on variegated surface; decorated with leaf motif and at top, bands of white flowers with yellow centers. Ht. 16½ in. Has original* Grueby Pottery, Boston *paper label.*

90. *Vase. Inverted conical form in pottery with four-lobed rim, body relief molded in leaf form; green matte glaze over all. Ht. 7½ in. Marked* Grueby Faience Co. Boston U.S.A.

91. *Vase. Squat baluster form in pottery; variegated surface has deep crevices, mustard-color matte glaze. Ht. 3½ in. Marked* Grueby Faience Co. Boston U.S.A.

92. *Vase. Squat baluster form in pottery with variegated tan matte glaze. Ht. 3 in. Marked* Grueby Faience Co. Boston U.S.A.

93. *Carriage clock. Rectangular box form in pewter with bail-carrying handle on top; copper dial enameled in blue and green. Ht. 4½ in. Carries* TUDRIC *mark of Liberty of London.*

94. *Coffret. Small rectangular box of wood cased in silver, on four splayed feet; top decorated in polychrome enamels beneath silver tree-branch motif; elaborate designs in silver over all. Ht. 3 in. Marked* CA *monogram of English designer Charles Rovert Ashbee.*

95. *Mantel clock. Curvilinear spear-point form of wood covered with repoussé copper; pewter face, copper hands; over-all thorn motif set with opalescent and colored glass cabochons; jutting curvilinear leg on back; key-wind works. Ht. 16½ in. Marked* Cuivres S. Bing Alf. Daguet *for French designer Daguet working for Parisian dealer S. Bing.*

96. *Candlestick. Cast bronze in form of nude woman leaning against poppy stem; candle cup in stylized poppy-pod shape, base in Art Nouveau linear motif; brown-green patina. Marked* RUBIN.

97. *Lamp. Iridescent yellow globe with mid-band of blue hooked decoration and overall rows of "zipper" motif; twin-pillared silvered-pewter standard in form of female figures holding moonstones, on octagonal pedestal. Ht. 23 in. Unmarked; globe by Loetz of Austria, standard attributed to Peter Behrens.*

98. *Vase. Bulbous conical pottery form with rough-textured surface; polychrome iridescent glaze over all. Ht. 19 in. Marked* Pewabic Detroit.

99. *Table lamp. Leaded glass shade in triangular form, decorated with green-and-yellow wheat motif; bronze standard also in triangular form, but elongated, with matching decoration; three ball feet. Ht. 21½ in. Unmarked but attributed to Handel & Co.*

100. *Vase. Shouldered and ribbed pottery form with high exterior glaze shading from brown to orange, decorated with underglaze cherries and leaves in yellow, orange, and brown. Ht. 12 in.* Rookwood-Van Briggle *mark.*

101. *Vase. Elongated incurved bucket form with bubbly variegated green glaze over all. Ht. 7¼ in. Marked* DEDHAM Pottery M.

102. *Vase. Bulbous pottery form with short cylindrical neck, decorated with Indian portrait labeled* Wanstall Arapahoe *and signed* A.F.Best; *high exterior glaze shading from brown to orange. Ht. 11¾ in. Marked* OWENS UTOPIAN 1025.

103. *Ewer. Large shouldered baluster form in pottery with undulated trefoil mouth and applied ribbed handle extending from shoulder to neck; high exterior glaze shading from brown-green to yellow-orange, decorated with black-eyed Susans and leaves. Ht. 17 in.* Rookwood-Shirayamadani *mark.*

104. *Statuette. Standing female figure in exotic dress; bronze and ivory on marble base. Ht. 15 in. Marked* Joe Descomps *for French artist Joseph J. Emmanuel Descombs.*

105. *Vase. Inverted conical form in pewter with flared circular rim and four handles, two with blue enamel ovals at body connection, two with blue enamel triangles at rim connection. Ht. 6 in. Marked* ENGLISH PEWTER MADE BY LIBERTY & CO. 0864 MK

106. *Vase. Elongated baluster form in iridescent creamy-gold glass with two drawn loop handles at upper rim; band of dark-red and gold pulled decoration at bottom. Ht. 16¾ in. Attributed to Loetz (Austria); carries a fraudulent* L.C.T. *mark.*

107. *Vase. Elongated shouldered baluster form in white pottery with flared circular rim and cylindrical base; decorated with stylized blue, purple, brown, and green Art Nouveau iris-and-leaf motif; orange-yellow interior glaze. Ht. 19½ in. Marked* II.B 696.

The Room Settings: A Reminder

*M*ost art is made to be used, not collected. True, in recent times we have had "art" consisting of such things as a slip of paper handed to the patron as proof that the artist and the recipient engaged in conversation on a high plane. It also is true that museums display art in rows as though it were made for exhibition purposes. We must have art that challenges our ways of thinking, and hanging paintings in rows is an effective way to show them, but it is important to remember that a lot of art is made to take home. And, with the exception of his ecclesiastical art and gravemarkers, this is true of Tiffany's.

The room settings in this exhibit show how the objects can be used — to sit on, to light up a parlor, to hold books or flowers or to brighten up an alcove.

The Art Nouveau Room (No. 108) contains chairs and a tea table by Louis Majorelle; a ceramic vase by Clement Massier; glass vases by Tiffany, Steuben, and Loetz; a Loie Fuller lamp by Raoul Larche; a Tiffany Lily floor lamp; and two prints by Alphonse Mucha.

The Turn-of-the-Century Classic Room (No. 109) contains a white and gold chair from Tiffany's art museum at Laurelton Hall; A Tiffany portrait lamp, a Tiffany table lamp; Favrile glass accessories and a desk set by Tiffany; an oil landscape by J. G. Brown, an oil painting, "Mother and Child," by George de Forest Brush; a pastel by Arthur B. Davies; and an etching by Pierre Auguste Renoir.

The Craftsman Style Room (No. 110), contains a library table made by Chicago's Toby Furniture Company; a lamp by Elbert Hubbard's Roycrofters; a Lebolt silver bowl; chairs, a bookcase and a desk by Gustave Stickley; a smoking stand, student lamp, and desk set by Tiffany; a ceramic vase by Moorcroft; a Van Briggle ceramic vase; and vases by the Rookwood and Grueby Potteries.

The rooms also show how the art objects look when serving their original purpose, how they relate in style to each other, and how they change in appearance with a change of light.

Tiffany: A Pioneer in Photography

*L*ouis Comfort Tiffany's role as a pioneer in photography is not well-known, but in his own day he was often credited, along with the famous Englishman Eadweard Muybridge, with making early photographs of animals in motion. Tiffany also was intrigued with the motion picture camera and made films of grandchildren dancing in his gardens, an activity which gave him more pleasure than it did them. The photographs shown here are a record of his fascination, not only with animals in action but also with the patterns made by busy men, women, and children. Many of his subjects did not know they were being photographed, and Tiffany's interest in the charm of the unplanned composition is obvious.

Tiffany used photographs in many ways. His own served as sketches and studies for his paintings. His staff made photographic records of articles produced in his studios and furnaces. He used commercial photographs of scenes in Africa and the Middle East as source material for himself and his staff designers.

Tiffany was one of the first to recognize photography as an important art form, and in 1918 he carefully provided that the Louis Comfort Tiffany Foundation would grant fellowships to photographers as well as to painters, sculptors, and designers.

Photography

111. *A selection of photographs taken by Louis C. Tiffany.*

Fern Vase, Gold-Plated Copper (#114)

F ew serious painters of today would deign to design such things as desk sets or pin trays, but many painters of the Belle Epoque were busy making beautiful and useful objects. They were influenced to some extent by William Morris, England's eloquent artist-politician, but a general movement to make the arts a part of everyday life was in the air.

Tiffany and Morris thought alike in many ways, but whereas Morris dreamed of a new Middle Ages with guilds of artist-artisans happily making a limited number of beautiful objects, Tiffany thought in terms of the Industrial Revolution's production line. Between 1899 and 1928, the staff and workers of his Corona furnaces made tens of thousands of useful objects, all well designed and equally well made.

Tiffany's metalwares were mostly bronze finished in a variety of textures and colors. A limited number of lamp bases, ash trays, and bowls were covered with a mosaic of Favrile glass, and some of them (the enamels) were copper covered with a thin coat of colored glass. He also worked in silver and silverplate.

The metalwares raise this question: "Which were designed by Tiffany himself?" Most of the surviving designs (in watercolor and gouache) are marked "approved by L.C.T." and a few are signed by Tiffany. Many pieces have none of the characteristics of Tiffany's personal work. A good example is the delicate, classical Louis XVI desk set.

The "Chinese" pattern, on the other hand, has a bulky simplicity which points to Tiffany, as do most of the enamels and much of the silver marked "Tiffany Studios." His part in these may have been a simple sketch on a pad of paper which was then translated into a detailed drawing, or a wax model, by members of his staff. It is important to remember, however, that the thinking and the taste expressed in all the metalwares is essentially Tiffany's.

Enamels

112. *Tray. Flattened asymmetrical form, small compartment with swivel lid; gold-plated copper with molded pattern of milkweed pods, enameled in iridescent blue, green and brownish yellow. L. 11¼ in. Inscribed* Louis C. Tiffany E L 169 ~~349~~.

113. *Vase. Inverted, slightly conical form; gold-plated copper with molded design of maple leaves and seed pods; enameled in iridescent blue, purple, rose, and yellow-orange. Ht. 8¾ in. Inscribed* S/C82 L.C.T. *and* S G111; *engraved on base* F.A.C. from A.A.C. July 8th 1904.

114. *Vase. Cylindrical form; gold-plated copper with molded design of opening fern tendrils; enameled in iridescent mauve, gold, green, and blue. Ht. 9 in. Inscribed* Louis C. Tiffany SG80 S/C 249; *owners monogram engraved* FBC.

115. *Vase. Incurved bucket form; copper with random lava-type design; exterior enameled in iridescent dark blue green and orange-red, interior in iridescent pale orange. Ht. 7 in. Inscribed* Louis C. Tiffany E.L. 101 386 590/37, *owners monogram engraved* G.A.C.

116. *Covered box. Cylindrical form; gold-plated copper enameled pea green, with clear glass chunks melted into the domical cover. Ht. 1⁷⁄₁₆ in. dia. 3¹⁵⁄₁₆ in. Inscribed* 8589 11 590/27 Louis C. Tiffany.

117. *Pin tray. Flattened asymmetrical form; gold-plated copper with molded floral pattern; enameled in pink, red, green, and blue. L. 3 in. Inscribed* EL 246B 3 L.C.T.

118. *Miniature vase. Squat bulbous form; gold-plated copper; enameled blue with floral pattern in pink, green and red. Ht. 2⁷⁄₈ in. Inscribed* L.C.T. E.L. 19.

119. *Vase. Bulbous curvilinear form; copper with molded pattern of Dutchman's Pipes and leaves; enameled in iridescent blue, green, and orange-red. Ht. 7½ in. Inscribed* 162 A-Coll. L.C.Tiffany SG 123.

Tiffany Studio Metals

120. *Tea Kettle on stand with warming lamp. Curvilinear hexagonal form; silver-plated bronze with wood-handled bail, and wooden finial on lid. Ht. over all, 10¼ in. Marked* Tiffany Studios New York, S/C 6885, 3.

121. *Creamer. Hexagonal form; silver-and gold-plated copper with ebony handle; molded pattern of trillium flowers and leaves over all, the leaves with a brown patina. Ht. 3¼ in. Marked* Tiffany Studios New York.

122. *Pen-and-ink stand. Casket form; silver-plated bronze inset with iridescent green Favrile glass turtleback tiles on body and lid and fitted with gold iridescent Favrile glass bucket-shape ink cups; center-front stamp drawer has secret compartment. Ht. 4¼ in. Marked on base* Tiffany Studios New York 10388 TIFFANY STUDIOS NEW YORK 3664; *on ink cups,* L.C.T.; *and on lid,* 3664.

123. *Covered box. Rectangular form; copper filigree with brown patina, in floral pattern; backed with green-and-white streaky glass panels; four ball feet of copper. L. 6¾ in. Marked* TIFFANY STUDIOS NEW YORK S/C 5160.

124. *Loving cup. Trumpet form with three handles; gold-plated bronze decorated with molded panels, and polished squares of orange opaque Favrile glass "jewels" set in bands around the top and on the handles. Ht. 7 in. Marked* Tiffany Studios New York.

Tiffany Glass & Decorating Company

125. *Cast-bronze candelabrum.* Four S-shape arms joined at domed base and ending in reticulated waisted candle cups lined in green glass; base ornamented with four molded leaf forms above band of inset molded spherical green glass "jewels"; flat circular bobèches with bead-chain ornament. Ht. 12¼ in. *Marked* TGDCo *monogram,* Tiffany Studios New York D887.

126. *Planter.* Squat incurved bucket form of bronze cast in blossom-and-leaf motif on a ground of iridescent greenish-blue glass tesserae; cylindrical copper insert. Ht. 4 in. *Marked on planter* TGDCo *monogram,* Tiffany Studios New York 29117 BS/C 305 S/C 5407.

127. *Scarab lamp.* Molded iridescent green glass scarab-form shade in bronze bezel mounted on U-shape arm; domed molded-bronze base. Ht. 8½ in. *Marked* TGDCo *monogram, 269* Tiffany Studios New York.

Metal Candlesticks

128. *Root candlestick.* Cast-bronze reticulated waisted candle cup lined with green glass, on slender bronze shaft which splays tri-symmetrically into curvilinear root-like feet. Ht. 3 in. *Marked* Tiffany Studios.

129. *Bamboo candlestick.* Cast bronze in form of bamboo stalk, split and splayed to form base; saucer-topped bobèche. Ht. 10½ in. *Marked* Tiffany Studios New York 1205.

130. *Candlestick.* Cast bronze; reticulated waisted candle cup lined with green glass, on tall slender shaft; circular base. Ht. 20¾ in. *Marked* 5393 Tiffany Studios New York.

131. *Cobra candlestick.* Incurved bucket-form candle cup held by three prongs on curvilinear arm, handle in form of cobra's head, irregularly shaped base; all in gilded bronze. Ht. 8 in. *Marked* Tiffany Studios, New York 1203, *curvilinear* TS *monogram.*

132. *Candlestick.* Cast bronze; elongated spool-form reticulated candle cup lined with green glass on tripod base ending in scroll feet; beaded bobèche. Ht. 10½ in. *Marked* S1230.

133. *Candlestick.* Saucer-topped candle cup in iridescent gold glass decorated with encircling applied prunts, on tall slender bronze shaft; bronze base in Queen Anne's lace motif. Ht. 9½ in. *Marked* Tiffany Studios New York D 883.

134. *Cobra candlestick.* Same as No. 131.

135. *Candlestick.* Spherical decorated glass candle cup on bronze stem set with two spherical iridescent glass "jewels;" stem flares to form conical base set with sixteen iridescent-gold "jewels" and resting on sixteen peg feet. Ht. 16¼ in. *Marked* Tiffany Studios New York 1223.

136. *Candlestick.* Spherical candle cup set with iridescent green glass "jewels;" short stem ending in three splayed legs with bronze spheres near the tip of each; all in cast bronze. Ht. 8½ in. *Marked* Tiffany Studios New York 1202 6104.

137. *Candlestick.* Cast bronze; incurved bucket-form cup held by three prongs, on tall slender stem ending in flat circular base. Ht. 16¾ in. *Marked* Tiffany Studios New York 1212 2507.

138. *Candelabrum.* Cast bronze; three squat reticulated spherical candle cups lined with green glass branch from each of two low opposing arms; snuffer is contained within a tall shaft rising from center; domed oval base. Ht. 15 in. *Marked* TS *curvilinear monogram,* Tiffany Studios New York. 10088.

Tiffany Furnaces Metal Works

139. *Basket-shaped fruit bowl. Ribbed bucket form in iridescent opalescent-white and dark-blue glass; flared circular rim with doré brass bezel; bail handle of same material, enameled. Ht. 3 in. Marked* Louis C. Tiffany Furnaces Inc. Favrile LCT *monogram, 508 6409.*

140. *Bowl. Saucer form in doré bronze with flared circular rim decorated with alternating panels of polychrome enamel and insert twisted wire. Ht. 1 in., dia. 7¾ in. Marked* Louis C. Tiffany Furnaces, Inc. Favrile LCT *monogram, 413.*

141. *Inkstand. Square form in enameled doré bronze, decorated with geometric designs in pink and blue; insert of iridescent gold pressed glass with floral motif on rim. Ht. 2½ in. Marked* LCT *monogram;* Louis C. Tiffany Furnaces Inc. 357 3510; *on glass,* L.C.T.Favrile.

142. *Bud vase. Elongated trumpet form in iridescent gold glass, held in inverted trumpet-shaped base of doré copper decorated with gold and red enamel. Ht. 12 in. Marked* Louis C. Tiffany Furnaces, Inc. LCT *monogram, 150C 189; on glass,* L.C.T. Favrile.

143. *Compote. Saucer form with stepped base and flared rim, in doré bronze; decorated on rim with band of half circles in red, black, and turquoise enamel. Ht. 2½ in. dia. 8½ in. Marked* LCT *monogram,* Louis C. Tiffany Furnaces, Inc. Favrile 526.

144. *Bowl. Stepped inverted conical form in doré brass; wide pierced floral-motif rim in polychrome enamel. Ht. 1 in., dia. 8 in. Marked* LCT *monogram,* Louis C. Tiffany Furnaces Inc. Favrile 419.

145. *Bowl. Saucer form on pedestal base with curvilinear conical foot, in doré brass; two horizontal enamelled pierced-work handles in pink and green floral motif. Ht. 3 in. dia. 12½ in. Marked* Louis C. Tiffany Furnaces Inc. Favrile 522 7839.

146. *Vase. Inverted trumpet form with lower body in angular knop shape, in iridescent gold glass; held in stepped inverted trumpet-form base of doré brass with decoration of interlaced lines. Ht. 12¼ in. Marked* Louis C. Tiffany Furnaces Inc. 164 Ah = .

147. *Powder box. Ribbed elliptical form in creamy opalescent-white glass; slightly domed doré brass cover with polychrome enameling in starburst motif. Ht. 2¾ in. glass. Marked* 4413N Louis C. Tiffany Inc. Favrile.

148. *Covered box. Octagonal form in silver and enamel; pebbled borders decorated in turquoise enamel and repoussé work. Ht. 1¾ in. Marked* Tiffany Furnaces Sterling 239 S/C 289. *Cover marked* 239.

Desk Set Patterns

149. *"Ninth Century" pattern calendar frame. Paneled rectangular form in doré bronze with wire support in back; panels decorated with celtic motifs and set in green and blue glass cabochons. Ht. 4¾ in. Marked* Tiffany Studios New York 1618 4872.

150. *"Heraldic" pattern clock. Four-sided conical form with domical top, in silvered bronze; brass face, inset leather-textured panels painted blue and decorated with heraldic shields. Ht. 4½ in. Marked* Tiffany Studios New York 2061.

151. *"Grape" pattern pen holder. Doré brass frame and filigree in grape motif over streaky caramel and white sheet glass; small metal loops in front to hold pens, two scrolled metal feet in back. Ht. 5¼ in. Marked* Tiffany Studios New York 1003.

152. *"Adam" pattern pen tray. Rectangular tray with rounded ends, in doré bronze; decorated in fan garland, and floral motifs. Ht. 8¾ in. Marked* Tiffany Studios New York 2071 9145.

153. *"Pine Needle" pattern book ends. Expandable rectangular frame and filigree in copper, decorated in pine-needle motif; green and brown patina. Ht. 5¾ in. Marked* Tiffany Studios New York 1027.

154. *"Zodiac" pattern paper rack. Two-tier rectangular rack in silvered bronze, decorated with Celtic motif and signs of the Zodiac. Ht. 5½ in. Marked* Tiffany Studios New York 1009 3492.

155. "Chinese" pattern inkstand. Octagonal conical form with lid in bronze, decorated with linear Chinese motifs from the Chou Dynasty: clear-glass insert; brown patina. Ht. 4½ in. Marked Tiffany Studios New York 1753 478.

156. "Spanish" pattern inkstand. Oval form with conical lid, in doré bronze; decorated with two opposing molded forms of griffins, portrait medallions, and various symbols; clear glass insert. Ht. 4¼ in. Marked Tiffany Studios 1883 9625.

157. "Graduate" pattern ashtray and match holder. Rectangular recessed tray in bronze; at center, four-sided spool-shape riser supporting a rectangular match holder; decorated in geometric motif; brown patina. Ht. 3½ in. Marked Tiffany Studios New York 1814 77S.

158. "Venetian" pattern stamp box. Stepped rectangular form with cover, in doré bronze; ornamental curvilinear hinges and latch and all over decoration, including a frieze of ermine and other motifs derived from 16th Century Venetian leather work. Ht. 2 in. Marked Tiffany Studios New York 1645 10037.

159. "Bookmark" pattern playing-card case. Rectangular form with hinged cover, in doré bronze; cover decorated with trees and vines in high relief, body with printers' and publishers' typographical symbols. Ht. 4 in. Marked Tiffany Studios New York 882 S 5030.

160. "American Indian" pattern rocker blotter. Rocker form with flattened inverted-baluster handle, in bronze; decorated with two opposing stylized frogs' heads and American Indian linear motifs; brownish-gold patina. L. 4½ in. Marked Tiffany Studios New York 1191 9230.

161. "Nautical" pattern inkstand. Rectangular form with domical lid representing a scallop shell, in bronze; low-relief panels of sailing ships, small crabs at corners of lid, dolphins at stand corners; clear glass insert; brown patina. Ht. 2½ in. Marked Tiffany Studios New York 1842.

162. "Modeled" pattern inkstand. Conical form with domical cover, in doré bronze; raised geometric motif overall; clear glass insert. Ht. 2½ in. Marked Tiffany Studios New York 1132 9354.

163. "Abalone" pattern paperweight. Octagonal conical form with conical finial, in doré bronze; decoration of recessed linear leaf forms and abalone discs representing grape clusters. Ht. 2 in. Marked Tiffany Studio New York 1162.

164. "Royal Copper" pattern utility box. Hand-formed and riveted rectangular form with cover, in sheet copper; red enamel finish with cloisonné symbols of the Zodiac. L. 3¾ in. Marked Tiffany Studios New York 1771.

165. "Louis XVI" pattern blotter ends. Curvilinear and straight-sided forms in doré bronze decorated with delicately molded sea shells and scrollwork. L. 12¼ in. Marked Tiffany Studios New York 1820. Marked 10034.

"Abalone" Pattern Desk Set

166.-182. "Abalone" pattern desk set. All pieces in doré bronze set with discs of abalone shell in grape motif, and all are marked Tiffany Studios New York with the additional of the numbers indicated below:

a.	Paper rack	1151/2949
b.	Blotter ends	1152/2812
c.	Inkstand	1157/2780
d.	Stamp box	1158/5307
e.	Pen tray	1159/2020
f.	Pen brush	1160/ 867
g.	Paper knife	1163/3196
h.	Rocker blotter	1164/7119
i.	Letter clip	1165/1296
j.	Calendar frame	1166/1390
k.	Thermometer	1167/ 925
l.	Memoranda pad	1169/1376
m.	Letter scales	1170/2371
n.	Utility box	1176/1845
o.	Reading glass	1178/1368
p.	Lampshade	1928/1855
q.	Lamp base	604/4456

The Lampshades: Began with the Chapel

Nautilus Lamp (#195)

O
ne feature of Tiffany's Columbian Exposition Chapel was a circular window eight feet across after a painting by Botticelli. The window is still in the original wood mount, complete with a sheet of diffusing glass, indicating that Tiffany showed it backlighted with electric lights. Edison had introduced his electric light bulb in 1880. Tiffany and Edison had worked together on lighting New York's Lyceum Theater with electricity in 1885, and Tiffany was quick to see the potentials of the new lighting medium.

The baptismal font was covered with a leaded glass dome made the same way he would make lampshades later on. A giant "electrolier" made of gilded pipe and green turtleback tiles with light bulbs behind them provided most of the light in the Chapel.

It is not too difficult to guess what was going through Tiffany's mind while he was working on that project. Electric lighting was the way of the future, but bulbs did shine in your eyes. However, thought Tiffany, leaded glass is beautiful lighted with electric lights, and the leaded glass dome on the baptismal font would look good with a bulb in it.

Six years later, Tiffany was making leaded lampshades. He patented the Nautilus in 1899. The Dragonfly, designed by Clara Driscoll, a brilliant woman on Tiffany's staff, won a medal at the 1900 Paris International Exposition. Within a few years, the Tiffany Studios were making shades in 500 different patterns.

Many Tiffany lampshades are the work of Tiffany's staff designers, but some are from his own designs. One of the latter is the inverted dome from the dining room of Laurelton Hall, which repeats the pattern he had introduced into the blue rug beneath it. The green turtleback lamps from Laurelton Hall also are his. Other lamps, including the Wisteria and Spider, have the character of his own designs.

Turtleback Mosaic Lamp (#187)

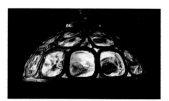

Dragonfly Lamp (#196)

As to the rest, it is important to remember that Tiffany was a determined, demanding taskmaster. The phrase "made under the personal supervision of Louis C. Tiffany," which appears repeatedly in advertisements and brochures of the Tiffany Studios, meant what it said.

The shades designed by his staff artists do reflect the taste of the designer, as well as the taste of the women who decided on the color, selected the pieces of glass, and leaded them together. But all Tiffany shades are ultimately Tiffany's, because they were made under the personal supervision of a remarkable man who worked it out so his employees wanted to do exactly as he wished.

Electricity Was New

183. *Cameo table lamp. Trumpet shape standard and domical shade of white glass cased in iridescent green, metal bulb-and-shade holder; wheel-carved decoration of white flowers on shade. Ht. 14½ in. Marked* L.C.Tiffany-Favrile *on the base and shade, plus* 2356K *on shade.*

184. *"Arabian" desk lamp. Conical shade on inverted-baluster standard, domed and folded foot, all in iridescent green glass; "Murano" decoration with vertical rows of zipper pattern over all; three pearl-gray French knots on standard and finial. Ht. 14 in. Marked* L.C.T. Favrile *on shade,* L.C.Tiffany-Favrile *on base.*

185. *Pair of hanging globes from the living room at Laurelton Hall. In three sections: top section reticulated bronze; center set with band of iridescent green turtleback tiles, lower section composed of white and green curvilinear leaded glass panels; hinged discs of opal-orange at bottom. Ht. 14 in. Unsigned.*

186. *Spider Web table lamp. Multicolored domical octagonal shade decorated with spider webs and apple blossoms, supported by bronze vines rising from a bronze standard set with mosaic tiles in narcissus pattern. Ht. 30 in. Unsigned.*

187. *Turtleback hanging lamp, one of three from the living room at Laurelton Hall; en suite with 56-44 a. and b. Iridescent green turtlebacks, tiles and chunks in bronze and leaded frame; lined with domical white glass diffuser. Ht. 13 in. Unsigned.*

188. *Bamboo floor lamp. Molded bronze standard in bambo-stalk form; domical leaded-glass shade depicting green bamboo foliage and ochre stalks on amber ground. Ht. 63 in. Marked on shade* Tiffany Studios New York; *on base,* Tiffany Studios New York 10923.

189. *Tulip table lamp. Shade decorated with design of orange-red tulips on mottled green ground; bronze "Grecian urn" standard. Ht. 22½ in. Marked on shade* Tiffany Studios New York; *on font,* Tiffany Studios 1453 *and* TGDCo *monogram.*

190. *Laburnum table lamp. Domical leaded glass shade has yellow and amber blossoms descending to undulated rim, all on bluish-lavender ground; pillared bronze standard. Ht. 32 in. Marked on shade* Tiffany Studios New York 1539; *on base,* Tiffany Studios New York 529.

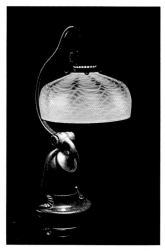

Counterbalanced Student Lamp (#191)

191. *Counterbalanced student lamp. Domical shade of iridescent greenish-gold glass with "Murano" decoration over white; curvilinear bronze standard with globular counterbalance weight. Ht. 15½ in. Marked on shade L.C.T. 5207; on base, Tiffany Studios New York 416.*

192. *Spider lamp. Hexagonal shade of coppered opalescent mottled yellow glass topped with six articulated ribs resembling spider's legs; bronze standard in form of inverted mushroom cap and stem. Ht. 18 in. Marked on shade Tiffany Studios New York 1424; on base Tiffany Studios New York 337.*

193. *Black-eyed Susan hanging lamp. Domed cylindrical leaded shade with yellow and amber black-eyed Susans, green leaves, and latticework on ground of fractured glass. Dia. 25 in. Marked Tiffany Studios New York.*

194. *Lotus table lamp. Shallow conical leaded shade with undulated rim, in opal and green glass; bronze standard with rayed base on ball feet. Ht. 24½ in. Marked on shade Tiffany Studios New York; on base, Tiffany Studios New York and TGDCo monogram, D795 25/66.*

195. *Nautilus table lamp. Leaded green and white glass shade in form of Nautilus shell, mounted in Y-shape bronze standard on domical base decorated with encircling leaf motif. Ht. 13½ in. Base marked Tiffany Studios New York and TGDCo monogram, 21345.*

196. *Dragonfly table lamp. Leaded glass shade rimmed with dragonflies with red bodies and reddish-amber wings, on yellowish-green background embellished with green "jewels;" bronze standard has ornamental wirework in form of descending tendrils; base decorated with rayed leaf design. Ht. 17 in. Marked on shade Tiffany Studios New York 1495; on base, 262 Tiffany Studios New York.*

197. *Miniature Wisteria table lamp. Cylindrical base composed of wisteria blossoms in various shades of blue and lavender with green leaves, pendant from open network of branches at slightly domed top; bronze standard in form of tree trunk covered with vines. Ht. 16¾ in. Marked on shade Tiffany Studios New York; on base, Tiffany Studios New York 7805.*

198. *Wisteria table lamp. Full-size lamp similar in form and design to 69-8 but in somewhat paler coloring and with less detailed tree-trunk standard. Ht. 27 in. Marked on shade Tiffany Studios New York 2076 TGDCo monogram, 27770.*

199. *Small table lamp. Domical opal-white shade decorated with iridescent gold "Murano" motif, on doré bronze standard in inverted-baluster form; ribbed domical base. Marked on shade L.C.T. Favrile 5; on base, LCT monogram, Louis C. Tiffany Furnaces, Inc. Favrile 16A.*

200. *Lily table lamp. Ten curvilinear branch-like arms in bronze terminating in iridescent gold trumpet-form shades and rising from bronze base of lily pads, buds, and blossoms in high relief; brown patina. Marked on shades L.C.T.; on base, Tiffany Studios New York 381.*

201. *Peony table lamp. Domical leaded glass shade with incurvate lower band, depicts peony blossoms shading from crimson to white with green foliage against an amber and blue ground. Originally from the estate of Louis Tiffany's son, Charles L. Tiffany.*

202. *Scarab desk lamp. Iridescent green mold-pressed glass scarab set in bronze bezel and mounted in bronze yoke atop a domed pedestal with ribbed perimeter; five annular shape bronze feet. Base marked 269 Tiffany Studios New York, TGDCo monogram.*

*T*iffany's art glass raises
questions: *Why did he want to make blown glass? When were the first pieces
made? Did Tiffany make any of the glass himself? Did he have secret formulas?
What do the marks mean?*

Blue Lily Vase, Favrile Glass, 1902

*One reason Tiffany turned to art glass was his desire to
make beauty available to as many people in as many forms as possible. The
wonderful discoveries he had made in his search for better glass for his windows
were another reason. He wanted to use that beautiful material in as many ways
as possible.*

*He also was interested in art as a business. Americans in the
last decades of the 19th Century were opening up the west, building railroads
and factories, making a lot of money, buying a lot of decorative art. Tiffany
believed he could sell art glass, and if in so doing he could raise the taste level
of the country, that would be just fine.*

*Another factor in Tiffany's work with art glass was his love
of color. As a traditional painter determined to record what the eye sees, he did
not use pure reds, blues, and greens as they came from the tube because all the
colors in nature are grayed a little by the atmosphere. In glass, it was different.
He could and did use any color he wanted. He was free.*

*It is difficult to say just when Tiffany made his first art glass.
The year 1893 is the commonly accepted date and he himself dated his first work
from that year. But there are those mysterious pieces signed "GTC," mysterious
because those are the initials of the Tiffany Glass Company, which became the
Tiffany Glass and Decorating Company in 1892. It would not be like Tiffany to
sign glass with the initials of a corporation no longer in existence. It is true he
had experimented with making glass in two commercial glasshouses in the 1870s
and 1880s, and for two years (1878-80) he owned his own glasshouse. The
pieces marked "GTC" could mean he was making art glass before 1893, and that
would be contrary to "the record." His Corona glasshouse was not in operation
until 1893.*

41.

Tiffany did not make the thousands of pieces of Favrile art glass himself, but it is all his in one sense. He visited his glasshouse regularly; he knew how to make and handle glass; he could predict with uncanny accuracy what a bubble of white hot glass would look like when it was blown and decorated; he was quick to spot the potentials in what a worker might consider a mistake; he gave directions to his workers by way of quick sketches; he broke pieces that did not meet his high standards. All his art glass reflects Tiffany's thinking, his ingenuity, and his taste. Louis Tiffany gave Tiffany glass its "look."

Whether Tiffany had secret formulas is an interesting matter for speculation. He was secretive. He did close the doors while working on his glass formulas. His glass was so new, so remarkable, glass men could hardly believe it. He did study chemistry on his own. He did mix batches and make glass himself. His window glass does cut better than any other glass. But he did employ a full-time chemist to help him, and his workers did know at least some of his formulas. And, of course, the workers did shovel the batch (mixture of ingredients) into the furnaces. Tiffany's secret may have been his ingenuity, his perserverance, his ability to organize and to lead.

The glass in Tiffany's art glass is made of powdered silica rock (about 50%), red lead (about 30%), pearl ash (about 15%), small amounts of other ingredients such as arsenic, and the metallic oxides which, by serving as filters, determine its colors. This is the soft, heavy, brilliant "crystal" which rings when when thumped. The lime glass in his windows is roughly: silica (about 70%), lime (about 15%), and soda (about 10%). Window glass is harder and lighter. It is possible Tiffany may have added "other ingredients" that no one knew about to some of his special batches.

The marks of Tiffany's art glass have fascinated and frustrated students and collectors for years. Many explanations are available, but none answers all the questions. It seems clear that the first pieces made in the Corona glasshouse carried numbered paper labels; that the number on the paper label later also was engraved on the glass; and that when the numbers got too high, letters were used as prefixes and later as suffixes. Attempts to assign a letter to a year have not proved satisfactory. It seems likely that the prefix or suffix changed any time the number reached 10,000.

A letter dated September 3, 1926, from the Tiffany Furnaces, "inventors and sole manufacturers of Favrile Glass" in Corona, Long Island, to Homer Eton Keyes, Editor of Antiques Magazine, *was published in part by that prestigious publication. It is reproduced here in its entirety because the complete letter throws light on this matter.*

It is available through the kindness of Edith Gaines, who served as Associate Editor of Antiques Magazine *and who has written the descriptions of the articles in this catalog.*

LOUIS C. TIFFANY FURNACES, INC.
INVENTORS AND SOLE MANUFACTURERS OF

FAVRILE GLASS
WORKERS IN METALS, ENAMELS AND GLASS

CORONA, LONG ISLAND, NEW YORK

CABLE ADDRESS "FAVRILE, NEW YORK" WESTERN UNION CODE

COLLECTIONS HAVE BEEN PURCHASED
AND ARE EXHIBITED BY THE PRINCIPAL
ART MUSEUMS OF THE WORLD

FOR PRIORITY OF INVENTION AND
ARTISTIC EXCELLENCE AWARDS OF THE
HIGHEST ORDER HAVE BEEN GIVEN

September 3, 1926.

Mr. Homer Eaton Keyes,
683 Atlantic Avenue,
Boston, Massachusetts.

Dear Sir:

Mr. Louis C. Tiffany has referred to the writer your letter of August 10th. The information you ask for could only be given in a rather lengthy communication but I will endeavor to reply as briefly as possible.

Tiffany Favrile Glass was invented in 1893 and was the result of Mr. Tiffany's desire to produce a glass which would serve as a medium for interpreting his ideas for Ecclesiastical windows. It was originally made only in sheet form for this purpose. Very shortly after its invention, however, Louis C. Tiffany developed an interest in blown glassware but he felt that in order to preserve the true characteristics of glass it should always be hand-made, hence the name "Favrile" under which it is known. This name is derived from an old Saxon word meaning hand wrought.

In reply to your inquiry regarding the letter N, this must be peculiar to the piece referred to. All articles of Favrile Glass are marked with the name or initials and all unusual pieces bear a number. The alphabet was first used by prefixing each number with the letter. For instance, the first piece of glass was numbered A 1 and the A series was continued until 9,999 pieces had been shipped when the B series was taken up. The entire alphabet has been used as a prefix and we are now using it as a suffix and are at present in series N. This does not mean that the number of articles represented by 9,999 times 40 is all that have been produced for many articles such as shades and tableware bear no letter at all and many of them bear no numbers. However, every article no matter how small nor how large bears the signature L.C.T. or the full name or such part of it as can be conveniently engraved upon the piece. We are enclosing two folders which describe in some measure the general character of our products and the method of marking them.

I trust that this gives you the information you desire.

Yours very truly,

A. Douglas Nash

Glass: Floriform Vases

203. *Vase. Elongated triangular form, domed and folded foot; opal body with green feather motif. Ht. 12 in. Marked L.C.T. Y6535 and has original LCT monogram paper label.*

204. *Vase. Inverted conical cup on slender stem, domed and folded foot; opal and clear glass cup with pink-ochre and green flame motifs, iridescent orange foot with green feather motifs, and pale gold iridescent interiors. Ht. 12½ in. Marked L.C.T. M 1155 and has original TGDCo monogram paper label.*

205. *Vase. Blossom form solid flattened conical foot; semi-opaque chartreuse body, transparent chartreuse foot. Ht. 5½ in. Marked L.C.Tiffany-Favrile. 1938.*

206. *Vase. Jack-in-the-pulpit form, bulbous base; white body, gold at top, vertical green stripes on stem, iridescent over all. Ht. 13 in. Marked L.C.T. M2068 and has original TGDCo monogram paper label.*

207. *Vase. Jack-in-the-pulpit form; iridescent gold throughout. Ht. 18½ in. Marked 3918G L.C.Tiffany-Favrile.*

208. *Vase. Inverted conical form fluted top, bulbous base; opal upper body with green flame motif, clear and green lower body with band of brown feather motif; pale iridescence over all. Ht. 11¼ in. Marked L.C.T. M 2251 and has original TGDCo monogram paper label.*

209. *Vase. Tulip form, domed and folded foot; opal body with orange-gold flame motif, green feather motif on foot, iridescent over all. Ht. 13¼ in. Marked L.C.T. M525 and has original TGDCo monogram paper label.*

210. *Vase. Thistle form, domed and folded foot, elongated solid stem; pale to bright orange iridescent areas on body and foot, white and green feather motif on body and stem. Ht. 14 in. Marked L.C.T. B786.*

211. *Vase. Elongated Jack-in-the-pulpit form, bulbous base; iridescent pale green top and interior, opal and green vertical stripes on stem. Ht. 19 in. Marked L.C.T. T 1146.*

Glass-Tiffany Glass Company-Monogram

If the initials GTc acid etched on the bottom of these pieces stand for Tiffany Glass Company, this glass presents a problem for art historians. The Tiffany Glass Company was dissolved in February 1892. The commonly used date for Tiffany's first art glass is 1893.

212. *Vase. Elongated bulbous form; white body with two rows of iridescent gold feather motif; iridescent gold interior. Ht. 10 in. Mark: GTc acid etched monogram.*

213. *Vase. Small baluster form; iridescent creamy-tan body with goldish-brown and gold feather motif. Ht. 4 in. Mark: GTc acid etched monogram.*

214. *Vase. Small baluster form; blue-black body with random trailing of gold, gold interior; iridescent throughout. Ht. 2¾ in. Mark: GTc acid etched monogram.*

215. *Vase. Incurved spool form; iridescent creamy-green glass body with over-all brown optic pulled design and large green heart-shaped leaves. Ht. 7½ in. Mark: GTc acid etched monogram.*

216. *Vase. Baluster form, undulated base area; iridescent blue-black body with random trailings of iridescent gold and iridescent gold interior. Ht. 7½ in. Mark: GTc acid etched monogram.*

217. *Bowl. Inverted conical form with undulated rim; iridescent white glass body with gold and green feather motif. Ht. 3 in. Mark: GTc acid etched monogram.*

Lava Glass

218. *Vase. Bulbous semi-cylindrical form; iridescent deep-amber body with variegated cobalt-blue crust, aplied iridescent gold spiral band and small random areas of gold. Ht. 7½ in. Marked 9771K L.C.Tiffany-Favrile.*

219. *Vase. Conical form; iridescent gold body with variegated cobalt-blue crust, applied iridescent gold spiral band. Ht. 5 in. Marked 328C L.C.Tiffany-Favrile.*

Glass Marked A-Coll.

Tiffany had a collection of his own work. The pieces were marked "A-Coll." for artist's collection. The simple little vase marked "A-Coll. No. 1" must be the first piece of glass in this collection. It has the simplicity he liked and is made of window glass which is harder than the "crystal" used in his "art glass."

220. *Beaker. Molded cylindrical form, two rows of convex shapes encircling base; dark-amber and opaque creamy-tan body; slight iridescence over all. Ht. 5 in. Marked 109 A-Coll. L.C.Tiffany-Favrile.*

221. *Vase. Angular faceted form; body dark blue and marbleized green and creamy tan. Ht. 3½ in. Marked 104 A-Coll. L.C.Tiffany-Favrile.*

222. *Paperweight. Pyramid form; opaque and dark-amber body; all surfaces polished. Ht. 2½ in. Marked 97 A-Coll. L.C.Tiffany-Favrile.*

223. *Vase. Inverted-baluster form; opaque white and translucent iridescent-clear body. Ht. 8 in. Marked 1 A-Coll. L.C.Tiffany-Favrile.*

224. *Vase. Baluster form; amber with random trailing of blue, pink, and green cased with clear; iridescent interior. Ht. 7 in. Marked 111 A-Coll. L.C.Tiffany-Favrile.*

225. *Wall Disc. Saucer shaped form of iridescent gold and clear with wheel cut concentric bands at center and green and gold "zigzag" motif on rim. Diam. 15½ in. Marked 206 A-Coll. L.C.Tiffany-Favrile.*

Aquamarine Glass

This glass is sometimes called "paperweight," a term Tiffany did not use. The original idea was to suggest the beauty that can be seen through a glass-bottom boat.

226. *Vase. Bulbous shouldered form; pale transparent amber body, with heart-shaped green leaves and bluish purple and pink morning-glory blossoms cased in clear; iridescent interior. Ht. 6½ in. Marked L.C.T. Y 3193.*

227. *Vase. Waisted baluster form; solid bulbous base; clear body with inset ochre and creamy-white multi-petal blossom. Ht. 10¼ in. Marked 5254G L.C.Tiffany-Favrile.*

228. *Vase. Shouldered ovoid form; brownish-orange body with brown vines and purple-blue morning-glory blossoms cased in clear; iridescent orange interior. Ht. 8 in. Marked L.C.T. Y3092 and has original L.C.T. monogram paper label.*

229. *Pedestal bowl. Squat waisted bowl on solid conical form, flared base area; pale-blue body with water-lily blossoms and pads inside bottom of bowl, with stems descending to base. Ht. 7. in. Marked 5197G L.C.Tiffany-Favrile.*

230. *Vase. Elongated spool form; clear body with encircling white narcissus blossoms and green leaves cased in clear; iridescent interior. Ht. 12 in. Marked 8027K L.C.Tiffany-Favrile and has original L.C.T. monogram paper label.*

231. *Vase. Elongated inverted-baluster form; clear body with encircling cased design of yellow daffodils and green leaves; iridescent interior. Ht. 15½ in. Marked 8032K L.C.Tiffany-Favrile.*

Cypriot Glass

Cypriot glass comes in many colors but it all has a roughly textured finish.

232. *Vase. Massive spherical form with cylindrical neck; rough iridescent surface over all with random trenched pattern. Ht. 17½ in. Marked 2222 ~~1710~~ L.C.T. E150.*

233. *Vase. Inverted-baluster form; creamy gold iridescent body with rough brown hooked decoration around top. Ht. 6 in. Marked L.C.T. K241 Favrile-Exhibition Pieces.*

234. *Vase. Massive elongated-baluster form; clear body, spattered with dark orange and white hooked into random feather-like motif, near top. Ht. 24 in. Marked L.C.T. E118 ~~2395~~ 2218 and has original LCT monogram paper label.*

235. *Vase. Massive inverted-baluster form; deep pea-green body with over-all hooked decoration in iridescent gold and bubbly brown. Ht. 21¼ in. Marked L.C.T. E161 2217 ~~1709~~ and has original TGDCo monogram paper label.*

236. *Vase. Irregular ovoid form; bubbly orange-white body with flame-like hooked decoration in iridescent gold extending upward from base. Ht. 7¾ in. Marked* Louis. C. Tiffany L.C.T. E1771 *and has original TGDCo monogram paper label.*

237. *Vase. Flattened-knop form; greenish-gold body with rough exterior and applied greenish-gold pulls swirling from top to base. Ht. 3 in. Marked* 03167 *and has parts of original TGDCo monogram and Bing Art Nouveau paper labels.*

238. *Vase. Bulbous inverted-baluster form; dark-brown bubbly iridescent body with iridescent gold flame shapes extending from base toward top. Ht. 8½ in. Marked* L.C.T. K 1462 2461.

Exhibition Pieces

239. *Vase. Baluster form; body of creamy opal; partial casing of dark green with hooked decoration in iridescent gold. Ht. 5½ in. Marked* 84K L.C.Tiffany-Favrile Exhibition Piece.

240. *Vase. Elongated gourd form, optic ribbed, with small conical foot; red body, dark red base. Ht. 12 in. Marked* 100K L.C.Tiffany-Favrile Exhibition Piece.

241. *Vase. Squat baluster form on inverted-cone base; chartreuse glass cased in green and cameo-carved in encircling leaf motif. Ht. 5¾ in. Marked* 5540M L.C.Tiffany-Favrile Exhibition Piece.

242. *Vase. Waisted baluster form; heavy clear glass with cream-and-brown blossom in solid base area. Ht. 23 in. Marked* 5399M L.C.Tiffany Inc.-Favrile Panama-Pacific Ex.[n]

243. *Vase. Elongated conical form; dark amber decorated with white blossoms and dark-green leaves, cased in clear. Ht. 12½ in. Marked* 1146L L.C.Tiffany-Favrile Exhibition Piece.

244. *Vase. Waisted inverted-baluster form with bulbous neck; body green, neck iridescent amber with green and orange interlocking "zigzag" motif. Ht. 7¼ in. Marked* 2400J L.C.Tiffany-Favrile Panama-Pacific. Ex[w].

245. *Vase. Bulbous inverted-baluster form; iridescent blue body with carved leaves and stem at shoulder area. Ht. 7 in. Marked* 618G L.C.Tiffany[Inc.] Favrile Exhibition Piece *and has original LCT monogram paper label.*

246. *Vase. Inverted-baluster form of iridescent gold glass with irregular inclusions of blue and green cased with clear. Ht. 7¾ in. Marked* 8568H L.C.Tiffany Favrile, Paris Salon 1914.

Special Order Glass

The small "o" used as a prefix to the number is generally thought to designate pieces made to fill a special order.

247. *Inkwell. Heavily ribbed knop form; iridescent blue body with white hooked Damascene motif over all; silver neck ring with silver hinged cover decorated with abstract floral motif. Ht. 4⅘ in. Marked* L.C.T. o8476 *on glass.* Tiffany & Co. Maker Sterling Silver *on silver.*

248. *Vase. Ball-knop form with short cylindrical neck; opaque creamy body decorated with blue, gold, and brown "zipper-like" motif. Ht. 2¾ in. Marked* L.C.T. o9965 *and has original TGDCo monogram paper label.*

249. *Floriform vase. Incurved conical form on narrow stem, domed foot; iridescent amber throughout with white and red feather motif. Ht. 9¼ in. Marked* L.C.T. 07731.

250. *Vase. Shouldered baluster form, conical foot; translucent iridescent ochre with band of tooled iridescent silver blue. Ht. 10 in. Marked* Louis C. Tiffany o10515.

251. *Vase. Bulbous inverted-conical form with cylindrical neck; iridescent translucent ochre body with bands of iridescent gold and yellow hooked pattern at shoulder. Ht. 10 in. Marked* L.C.T. o7399.

252. *Bowl. Incurved bucket form; clear body decorated with rococo carving and red blossoms and green leaves in the Marquetry technique. Ht. 7 in. Marked* Louis C. Tiffany o3440 *and with original TGDCo monogram paper label.*

253. *Wall disc. Curvilinear sauced shape of iridescent green glass w/gold pulled decoration and wheel carved center boss. Marked:* Louis C. Tiffany o9170.

Tableware

254. *Compote. Flattened waisted form on long stem with swelling knop above domed and folded foot; gold iridescent throughout. Ht. 11 in. Marked* W8165 *and has original LCT monogram paper label.*

255. *Punch cup. Waisted cup on elongated conical stem; iridescent blue throughout with tooled and twisted surface areas. Ht. 3¾ in. Marked* L.C.T. W618.

256. *Champage glass ("Princess" pattern). Bowl in waisted ogee form on bladed knop, elongated inverted-baluster stem, and domed foot. Ht. 8 in. Marked* L.C.T. 619.

257. *Champagne glass. Same as GX, 3 with minor variatons. Marked* L.C.T.-Favrile-L.C.T. 1268B.

258. *Sherry glass ("Royal" pattern). Bell-form bowl on twisted two-part stem, conical foot; iridescent gold throughout. Ht. 5½ in. No mark.*

259. *Sherry glass ("Prince" pattern). Lipped bowl on slender stem, conical foot; iridescent gold throughout. Ht. 5½ in. Marked* L.C.T. T4871.

260.-261. *Finger bowl and underplate. (a) Bowl in conical form with ruffled rim; (b) flared circular plate with slightly ruffled rim; both iridescent gold throughout. Bowl Ht. 2¼ in. dia. 6 in.; plate dia., 7 in. each marked* L.C.T. 8919 *and with original* LCT *monogram paper label.*

262. *Compote. Inverted-dome form on ring-shape stem. domed foot; iridescent gold throughout. Ht. 7¼ in. Marked* 384P LCT. Favrile.

263. *Champagne glass ("Savoy" pattern). Cup-shape bowl on baluster stem, ball knop, conical foot; iridescent gold throughout. Ht. 6½ in. Marked* L.C.T. M9462.

264. *Salt dish. Squat lipped form with two handles, on four peg feet; iridescent gold throughout. Ht. 6½ in. Marked* L.C.T.

265. *Salt dish. Squat lipped form on four peg feet; iridescent gold throughout. Ht. 1½ in. Marked* M8561.

266. *Salt dish. Squat incurved saucer form, ruffled rim; iridescent gold throughout. Ht. 1 in. Marked* L.C.T. 210.

267. *Finger bowl. Incurved bucket form, heavily ribbed; crackled clear exterior; iridescent interior. Ht. 2¾ in. Marked* L.C.T. D1507.

268. *Sherry glass ("Flemish" pattern). Spool form, band of symmetrical threading at midbody; iridescent gold throughout. Ht. 3 in. Marked* T2506 L.C.T. *and has original* L.C.T. *monogram paper label.*

269. *Liqueur glass, from a set of six. Lipped bucket form on slender stem, conical foot; iridescent gold throughout. Ht. 4¾ in. No mark.*

270. *Same as 54-53 f, but marked* L.C.T.Favrile.

271. *Same as 54-53 f, but marked* L.C.T.

272. *Same as 54-53 f, but marked* L.C.T. Favrile.

273. *Compote. Flattened waisted form on long stem with swelling knop above domed and folded foot; iridescent gold throughout. Ht. 11½ in. Marked* L.C.T. 3440 *and has original* LCT *monogram paper label.*

274. *Compote. Saucer-form bowl with fluted rim, on short cylindrical stem; conical foot; iridescent gold throughout. Ht. 4½ in. Marked* 2272H L.C.Tiffany-Favrile.

275. *Champagne glass ("Dominion" pattern). Cup-form bowl on twisted stem, conical foot; iridescent gold throughout. Ht. 5½ in. Marked* L.C.T. T3524.

276. *Finger bowl. Inverted conical form with cut panels encircling lower body; iridescent gold throughout. Ht. 2¼ in. Marked* L.C.T. Favrile ~~228~~ 228.

277. *Nut dish. Thistle form with ruffled rim, on four peg feet; iridescent gold throughout. Ht. 3 in. Marked* 6181E L.C.Tiffany-Favrile.

278. *Plate. Circular slightly inverted conical form; creamy opal center with applied wide green edge decorated in gold at rim. Dia. 9 in. Marked* X87 3970M L.C.Tiffany Inc. Favrile.

279.-280. *Finger bowl and underplate ("Prince" pattern). Cup-form bowl and saucer-form underplate, both iridescent gold throughout. Dia. of bowl, 5 in; of plate, 6 in. Marked* L.C.T. Favrile 216 *on bowl,* L.C.T. Favrile 639 *on plate.*

More Glass

281. *Vase. Baluster form with heavy false bottom; iridescent gold body with suggestion of texture, cased in clear; iridescent interior. Ht. 5¹/₂ in. Marked* L.C.T. Favrile V280.

282. *Vase. Inverted-baluster form, panel-faceted exterior; creamy opal background marbleized in yellow opal. Ht. 7 in. Marked* L. C.Tiffany-Favrile C251.

283. *Vase. Baluster form on stepped foot; deep blue-brown body encircled by irregular clear band edged in iridescent gold; area of random-shaped iridescent glass chips visible through clear sections; foot is iridescent blue. Ht. 19¹/₄ in. Marked* 3301 P L.C.Tiffany-Favrile *and has original* LCT *monogram paper label.*

284. *Vase. Bulbous form; iridescent orange-opal at top, mid and lower body decorated with iridescent clear and green damascene motif. Ht. 7¹/₂ in. Marked* L.C.T. L2 *and with original* TGDCo *monogram paper label.*

285. *Vase. Inverted-baluster form; panel-faceted neck and cut diamond motif on remainder of body; marbleized ochre, purple-gray, and green. Ht. 7¹/₂ in. Marked* L.C.Tiffany-Favrile 7008D.

286. *Vase. Short bulbous form; iridescent dark blue-black decorated with multiple panels of gold drag-loop motif and band of clear diamond shapes at mid body revealing cased iridescent-gold glass chips. Ht. 4¹/₂ in. Marked* Louis C. Tiffany-Favrile.

287. *Vase. Inverted-baluster form, spool-shaped neck; black glass exterior with diamond shapes of blue glass below shoulder; blue glass interior. Ht. 7¹/₄ in. Marked* 1972N Louis C. Tiffany ᴵⁿᶜ Favrile *and with original* LCT *monogram paper label.*

Red: A Difficult Color

The colors in glass are due to metallic oxides melted in the glass. Different metals screen out different parts of the spectrum. Red, a "difficult" color, can be gotten by either gold, copper or selenium.

288. *Decanter. Baluster form; iridescent dark blue with band of hooked gold decoration at bulbous area; at top, applied silver ornament set with garnets in form of two opposing peacocks with diamond eyes; ridged silver stopper in inverted-baluster form on chain set with pearls; stopper itself is topped with a sapphire. Ht. 4¹/₄ in. Marked* L.C.T. D689 *and with original* TGDCo *monogram paper label.*

289. *Flower arranging bowl and frog. Bowl in pan form with open cylinder raising in center; iridescent blue glass exterior, interior with orange and green lily-pad and vine decoration; frog, cylinder form with two bands of applied loopwork at top and midbody. Dia. of bowl, 10¹/₄ in.; Ht. of frog, 3 in. Bowl marked* 1807 9191M Louis C. Tiffany Furnaces-Inc-Favrile 543/C63; *frog,* 1685 L.C.T. Favrile.

290. *Vase. Bulbous inverted-baluster form, cylindrical neck; aquamarine technique, with green vines and white millifiori florets encased in clear; iridescent interior. Ht. 8 in. Marked* R2401 Louis C. Tiffany *and with original* TGDCo. *monogram paper label.*

291. *Vase. Squat inverted-baluster form with cylindrical neck and stepped foot; body red, neck and foot blue-green with white multi-strand "zig-zag" motif on neck. Ht. 5³/₄ in. Marked* L.C.Tiffany-Favrile 5973E.

292. *Vase. Squat bulbous form with small circular mouth; marbleized red, brick-red, and green. Ht. 4³/₄ in. Marked* L.C.T. 1460 *and with original* Tiffany Favrile Glass *and* 1460 *paper labels.*

293. *Vase. Baluster form; brownish opal on upper third, brick-red on remainder of body; raised brick-red prunts and random blue vines over all. Ht. 5¹/₂ in. Marked* 3684P L.C.Tiffany-Favrile *and with original* LCT *monogram paper label.*

294. *Vase. Shouldered gourd form, stepped foot; exterior orange-red, interior iridescent. Ht. 5¼ in. Marked L.C.Tiffany-Favrile 5576E.*

295. *Vase. Elongated bulbous form with flared circular rim; red throughout; surface carved from base toward top with leaf motif. Ht. 6 in. Marked 4732B L.C.Tiffany-Favrile.*

The Pastel Colored Glass

298. *Vase. Trumpet form on short inverted-baluster stem, domed foot; optid-ribbed body striped opalescent white and red iridescent glass; foot striped opalescent white and clear. Ht. 14½ in. Marked L.C.Tiffany-Favrile 1900.*

299. *Wine glass. Lipped bowl with ridged base on pillar-molded stem, domed optic-ribbed foot; cup translucent greenish-opal, stem clear, foot opalescent white and clear. Ht. 8 in. Marked L.C.Tiffany-Favrile.*

300. *Wine glass. Inverted-conical bowl on slender stem, optic-ribbed domed foot; bowl opalescent white and reddish purple, stem clear, foot opalescent white and clear. Ht. 6½ in. Marked L.C.Tiffany-Favrile.*

301. *Wine glass. Optic-ribbed, lipped bucket-form bowl, opalescent and clear, on multiform stem (from top): clear spool, ribbed green sphere, clear spool, ribbed green inverted baluster; optic-ribbed conical foot. Ht. 8 in. Marked L.C.T.Favrile 45.*

Rock Crystal

305. *Vase. Irregular form of rock crystal carved in bud-and-leaf motif. Ht. 7 in. Marked 115 L.C.Tiffany.*

296. *Vase. Shouldered baluster form, conical foot; red exterior, iridescent interior. Ht. 4¾ in. Marked 2191J L.C.Tiffany-Favrile and with original L.C.T. monogram paper label.*

297. *Vase. Inverted conical form, spool neck, solid conical foot; red body cased in blue-black with inclusions of pale blue; casing removed by polishing to reveal vertical stripes of the red. Ht. 6½ in. Marked 3990N L.C.Tiffany Inc. Favrile.*

302. *Goblet. Optic ribbed waisted bucket-form bowl, opalescent white and salmon pink, on multiform stem (from top): green spool, green ribbed sphere with iridescent interior, green spool, green ribbed inverted baluster; green ribbed domed and folded foot. Ht. 9 in. Marked L.C.T.Favrile.*

303. *Center bowl. Ribbed inverted conical form, wide undulated rim, conical foot; rim translucent opal white, body decorated in aquamarine technique with green leaves and blue morning-glory blossoms; foot clear. Ht. 3½ in. Marked L.C.Tiffany-Favrile 2057P.*

304. *Cake stand. Ribbed disc on thick cylindrical stem, conical foot; disc translucent opalescent white and green, stem opalescent white. Ht. 4 in. Marked 5-1580 L.C.Tiffany Inc. Favrile.*

The Jewelry: Was Louis Comfort Tiffany Connected With Tiffany & Company?

Peacock Necklace, Obverse (#306)

Peacock Necklace, Reverse

*T*he public image of famous figures is usually a little blurred and this is true of the Tiffanys. Uncertainty about the connection between Louis Comfort Tiffany and New York's Tiffany & Company is widespread and it is time to clear up the matter.

Charles Lewis Tiffany, who founded Tiffany & Company in 1837, was Louis Tiffany's father. Charles, a merchant prince in every sense of the word, was brilliant, energetic, public spirited, honest, and successful. When he died in 1902, he left a fortune equal to one hundred million of today's dollars.

Tiffany & Company made things of superior quality and sold them in splendid surroundings. The store was filled with fine silver and ablaze with rare gemstones. Tiffany's, through its "Blue Book," offered the finest pieces to customers on a high-toned mail order basis and gladly sent expensive items on approval. Tiffany jewelry was well-made, worth every penny of the large prices asked, and it mirrored the fashionable styles of the period.

Louis Tiffany also made jewelry, but his was different. His father was essentially a merchant. Louis was a dedicated champion of beauty. Charles was the diamond's best friend and the Tiffany Setting, which holds a single diamond high in the air so it can flash its light in all directions, was copied by his competitors.

Louis preferred colored stones, and often used the less expensive grades of these. His jewelry features emeralds with the color and beauty of a drop of water; his rubies are sometimes a pale, lovely inexpensive pink; his opals are often a delicate and moderately priced blue-green; he used moonstones and other semiprecious stones. But the settings are so creative that much of Tiffany's jewelry has the look of today.

Charles did not design the Tiffany & Company jewelry. Louis did design the Louis Tiffany jewelry, and it was displayed and sold on the sixth floor of Tiffany & Company's Fifth Avenue store, along with his leaded lamps, pottery, glass, and metalwares. But, whereas Louis Tiffany's glass and metalwares are marked with his name or initials, his jewelry is stamped "Tiffany & Company." Nearly always, that is. Some pieces are marked "Tiffany Studios." And the "Peacock Necklace," his favored and most famous piece of jewelry, bears no mark at all.

By 1894, Louis was a director of Tiffany & Company and after his father's death in 1902, he was made vice president and art director.

Jewelry

306. *Peacock Necklace. Gold necklace centered with medallion depicting a peacock in mosaic of opals, amethysts, and sapphires; pairs of repoussé gold rosettes on either side, set with topaz and demantoids, hang from tulip-form plaques each depicting in enamel a pair of confronting peacocks flanking a cabochon emerald on background of sapphires, amethysts, and rubies; above and below the central medallion a looped chain set with pearls and demantoids ends in an enameled gold wreath set with a topaz from which hangs a single ruby; reverse of principal medallion pictures flamingoes and flowers in enamel on gold. Length 10 in. Unsigned; designed by Louis Comfort Tiffany and executed by Julia Sherman.*

307. *Brooch. Large opal set in gold threads and filigree and flanked by demantoids and sapphires. L. 2³/₄ in. Marked* Tiffany & Co.

308. *Pin. Gold filigree set with five light topazes, large gem in center surrounded by four smaller cabochons. Dia. 1¹/₄ in. Marked* Tiffany & Co.

309. *Lady's ring. Eighteen-karat gold set with large oval lapis lazuli cabochon in framework of berries and leaves. Marked* Tiffany & Co.

310. *Lady's ring. Fourteen-karat gold and enamel set with large emerald-cut deep-yellow topaz. Marked* 14K Tiffany & Co.

311. *Pin. Gold scrollwork set with large oval lapis lazuli cabochon. L. 1¹/₄ in. Marked* Tiffany & Co.

312. *Bracelet. Gold and dark-blue enamel in double strand centered with medallion containing one large and four smaller lapis lazuli cabochons. L. 7¹/₂ in. Marked* Tiffany & Co.

313. *Brooch. Large peridot in gold and green enamel* plique à jour *setting. Marked* Tiffany & Co.

314. *Ring. Large black opal of oval shape set in pierce work 14K gold mount. This opal was originally Louis C. Tiffany's watch fob.*

The Dining Room at Laurelton Hall:
*Strawberries Topped With Cream, Steamer Clams
and A Preview of Things to Come*

*Table and Chairs from the Dining
Room at Laurelton Hall
(#316-319)*

*L*ouis Tiffany began every
summer morning with breakfast at the octagonal table shown in this exhibition.
The time was always 7:30 a.m., for he was as prompt as a clock and so was
everyone else at Laurelton Hall, even visiting grandchildren. It was easy to be
prompt at Laurelton Hall. The clock tower contained a set of Westminster
chimes, and the dining room's simple marble mantlepiece was set with three
instruments: one told the month, one the day, and one the hour. Even Tiffany's
pocket watch rang the hour and minutes on command.

Laurelton Hall was more than a great estate, it also was a
model farm with its own dairy herd, gardens, and greenhouses. As one might
expect from a wealthy man who enjoyed the good things in life, Tiffany's meals
were a splendid experience. Even when he ate alone, the table was set for four
because it looked better that way. One breakfast was strawberries topped with the
richest cream; another was steamer clams.

The table is the original color, a light gray of Tiffany's own
mixing. Both table and chairs have an Oriental flavor, as do the medallions in
the deep blue rug beneath them. The table was one of three. Two, progressively
smaller and octagonal in shape, were used for breakfast or lunch. A large
rectangular table in the center of the room was used only when there were
guests. The large inverted dome in the center of the dining room repeated the
design of the medallion in the rug beneath. The same design also appeared on
the wall covering and in the velvet on the chairs.

A View of the Dining Room at Laurelton Hall

The wisteria transoms were installed later over the glass doors opening on the garden. Wisteria vines, a Tiffany favorite, hung from wires strung over the part of the garden that could be seen from the dining room. The doors on the other side of the dining room gave a broad view of the harbor and had no wisteria tramsoms.

The dining room at Laurelton Hall with its glass doors (which were, in effect, glass walls), bright colors, and simplicity rooted in the Japanese tradition anticipated many developments in interior design to come later in the 20th Century.

Laurelton Hall Dining Room

315. *Medallion Carpet from the Dining Room at Laurelton Hall; after 1908. Wool; 25 ft. x 8 ft. 8 in. Unsigned. The ground of mazarine blue is decorated with three central medallions of floral and arabesque detail surrounded by stylized cranes with outstretched wings. This design was repeated in the lampshade overhead as well as the wall covering.*

316. *Dining Table, ca. 1904. Painted wood; Ht. 29½ x Diam. 71 in. Unsigned, designed by Louis C. Tiffany. Painted gray and of octagonal form overall, the top rests on a recessed drum having a flared skirt and eight angular cabriole legs.*

317.-319. *Three side chairs, ca. 1904. Painted wood; 43½ x 15 x 17 in. Unsigned; designed by Louis C. Tiffany. En suite with table (No. 316) and painted the same gray.*

320. *Arm chair, ca. 1904. Painted wood; 45 x 18 x 18½ in. Unsigned; designed by Louis C. Tiffany. En suite with the table (No. 316) and the chairs (Nos. 317-319) and painted the same gray.*

321. *Ceiling Light from the Dining Room, Laurelton Hall, after 1904. Favrile glass and forged iron; diam. 66 in. Unsigned. The shade of leaded pink, blue, purple, and amber Favrile glass repeats the central medallion in the rug. All solder joints are silvered.*

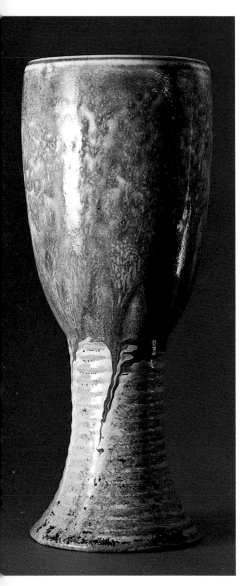

Why Pottery?

*T*iffany began making Favrile pottery at his Corona furnaces around the turn of the century. The simple shapes often represent growing things. The pottery is highly experimental in nature, and Tiffany may have, as one of his workers stated, designed all the Favrile pottery himself. (The trade name "Favrile" was applied to pottery as well as to his glass.)

Much of the art pottery made by his contemporaries was decorated with pictures of trees, flowers, literary characters, and Indians. The work was done at the pottery and it was all under the glaze. Tiffany's pottery was not designed to have pictures painted on it. It was to be enjoyed for itself, for the quality of the shape and the way it was finished. Some pieces are glazed (a thin coat of glass melted over the surface), some are bisque (fired but not glazed), and some are covered with a thin sheet of metal (bronze pottery), a technique he may have borrowed from Rookwood pottery.

Tiffany turned to pottery in his endless effort to infiltrate the American home with beauty and good taste. How successful the venture was is difficult to say. Not much was made and still less was sold. His pottery is one more illustration of Tiffany's being ahead of his time. Its simplicity and the imaginative ways it is glazed and finished make it look quite contemporary.

Vase. Stalk-of-Celery form. (#336)

Bronze Pottery

322. *Vase. Conical form; greenish-gray-gold exterior, clear interior glaze; raised trellis-band and poinsettia-leaf decoration. Ht. 16½ in. Marked* LCT *conjoined monogram, BP 190 B.P. 346 L. C. Tiffany-Favrile Bronze Pottery.*

323. *Vase. Incurved spool form; brown exterior, green interior glaze; raised water-lily leaf-and-stem decoration. Ht. 12¼ in. Marked* LCT *conjoined monogram, 7 BP 515 L. C. Tiffany-Favrile Bronze Pottery.*

324. *Vase. Shouldered baluster form; copper with silver exterior, green interior glaze; raised maple-leaf-and-stem decoration. Ht. 4¾ in. Marked* LCT *conjoined monogram, B.P. 298 L. C. Tiffany-Favrile Bronze Pottery.*

325. *Vase. Baluster shape; green-brown exterior, green interior glaze; raised arrowroot-leaf-and-flower decoration with intertwined snake. Ht. 8¼ in. Marked* LCT *conjoined monogram, L. C. Tiffany-Favrile Bronze Pottery B.P. 315 32 2328.*

326. *Vase. Cylindrical form; bronze exterior, green interior glaze; raised corn stalk decoration. Ht. 13 in. Marked* LCT *conjoined monogram, 7 L. C. Tiffany-Favrile Bronze Pottery B.P. 279 6262.*

327. *Vase. Annular form; gold-plated exterior, clear interior glaze; raised leaf, stem, and berry decoration. Ht. 2 in. Marked* LCT *conjoined monogram, BP 517 L. C. Tiffany-Favrile Bronze Pottery.*

328. *Vase. Ovoid incurved form; gold-plated exterior, green interior glaze; raised decoration of two small chicks and two groups of dandelions. Ht. 2¼ in. Marked* LCT *conjoined monogram, 7.*

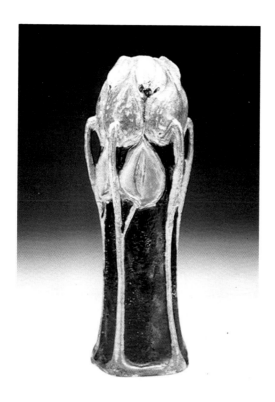

Ceramic Vase with Milkweeds (#341)

Artist's Collection

329. *Vase. Elongated ovoid form; iridescent blue-black, green, brown, and yellow running glaze on exterior, brown interior glaze. Ht. 14¾ in. Marked* LCT *conjoined monogram, 7 84 A-Coll. L. C. Tiffany-Favrile Pottery.*

330. *Vase. Three-handled bulbous form; variegated blue-green-gray running glaze on exterior, clear and blue-speckled interior glaze. Ht. 11 in. Marked* LCT *conjoined monogram, 7 201 A-Coll. L. C. Tiffany-Favrile Pottery.*

331. *Vase. Bulbous melon-ribbed form; yellow-green high glaze over all. Ht. 16¼ in. Marked* LCT *conjoined monogram, 7 82 A-Coll. L. C. Tiffany-Favrile Pottery.*

332. *Vase. Baluster form; dimpled aquamarine and cobalt-blue running glaze over all. Ht. 4 in. Marked* LCT *conjoined monogram, 127 A-Coll. L. C. Tiffany-Favrile Pottery.*

333. *Vase. Baluster form; crystal-stippled aquamarine and cobalt-blue glaze over all with one blood-red highlight at shoulder. Ht. 5½ in. Marked* LCT *conjoined monogram, B 183 A-Coll. L. C. Tiffany-Favrile Pottery.*

334. *Vase. Cylindrical form; silvered bronze exterior, greenish-white interior glaze; raised nasturtium-blossom-and-leaf decoration. Ht. 7¼ in. Marked* LCT *conjoined monogram, 40 A-Coll. L. C. Tiffany-Favrile Bronze Pottery BP. 325.*

335. *Vase. Tear-drop form; variegated green and blue-green semi-matte glaze over all. Ht. 7¾ in. Marked* LCT *conjoined monogram, 7 129 A-Coll. L. C. Tiffany-Favrile Pottery.*

Ceramic Vase

"Lava" Vase, Favrile Glass (#218)

Pottery Using Nature Forms

336. *Vase. Stalk-of-celery form; clear pale-green glaze over all. Ht. 11¼ in. Marked* LCT *conjoined monogram* P 1343 L. C. Tiffany-Favrile Pottery.

337. *Vase. Undulated conical form; transparent yellow-green high glaze over all with raised vine and pea-pod decoration. Ht. 9 in. Marked* LCT *conjoined monogram, 7.*

338. *Vase. Incurved spool form; greenish-yellow glaze over all; raised artichoke-leaf decoration. Ht. 11 in. Marked* LCT *conjoined monogram, 7.*

339. *Vase. Tree-stump form; ochre-brown exterior glaze, clear interior glaze; raised toadstool encircling decoration. Ht. 6 in. Inscribed* LCT *conjoined monogram, 7.*

340. *Vase. Baluster form; iridescent green and dark-green glaze over all; raised arrowroot-leaf-and-flower design with intertwined snake. Ht. 5½ in. Marked* LCT *conjoined monogram, 7.*

341. *Vase. Five-paneled cylindrical form; blue-black, green, gray-green, light blue, white, and brown glaze; raised milkweed-pod and stem decoration. Ht. 10 in. Marked* LCT *conjoined monogram, P AG.*

342. *Pitcher. Semi-flattened cylindrical form; ivory and medium to dark green glaze over all; raised cattail-and-leaf decoration. Ht. 12½ in. Marked* LCT *conjoined monogram, 7 P1157 L. C. Tiffany-Inc. Favrile Pottery.*

343. *Vase. Ovoid form; iridescent cream and brown glaze over all; raised leaf and flower-bud decoration over entire body. Ht. 5 in. Marked* LCT *conjoined monogram, 7.*

344. *Vase. Inverted-baluster form; semi-matte yellow-green glaze; raised blades-of-grass decoration. Ht. 7¾ in. Marked* LCT *conjoined monogram, 7 L.C.T.*

Bisque (unfired) Pottery

345. *Vase. Cylindrical form; raised calla-lily and leaf decoration. Ht. 11¼ in. Marked* LCT *conjoined monogram,* 7.

346. *Vase. Spherical form; white outer surface, green interior glaze; upper half in shape of incurved fern tendrils. Ht. 10½ in. Marked* LCT *conjoined monogram.*

347. *Vase. Flattened-knop form; band of incised and carved poinsettia leaves on upper body. Ht. 2½ in. Marked* LCT *conjoined monogram.*

348. *Vase. Inverted conical form; raised apple, leaf, and branch decoration over all. Ht. 8 in. Marked* LCT *conjoined monogram,* 7 P1458 L.C.T. *Pottery.*

349. *Flower holder. Incurved flattened form with pierced shoulder; molded decoration of vines and five-petaled blossoms. Ht. 2½ in. Marked* LCT *conjoined monogram.*

350. *Vase. Triangular vertical form; buff outer surface. Dark-green interior glaze; curled fern-tendril decoration. Ht. 9½ in. Marked* LCT *conjoined monogram,* 7.

Three Identical Pieces with Different Finishes and Other Pottery

351. *Bowl. Flattened ovoid shape; blue, green, aquamarine and clear running exterior, clear interior glaze; molded fish-and-wave design over all. Ht. 4½ in. Marked* LCT *conjoined monogram,* P EL *monogram.*

352. *Bowl. Identical with 351, except executed in bisque with green interior glaze. Marked* LCT *conjoined monogram,* 7.

353. *Bowl. Identical with 351 except cased in bronze with green interior glaze. Marked* LCT *conjoined monogram,* B. P. 392 L. C. Tiffany-Favrile *Bronze Pottery* 47.

354. *Vase. Three-handled bulbous form; variegated thick green, dark-green, and yellow-green matte glaze over all. Ht. 12½ in. Marked* LCT *conjoined monogram,* 7.

355. *Vase. Baluster form; bubbly ochre-green-brown glaze over all. Ht. 4¾ in. Marked* LCT *conjoined monogram,* B. 57F. EL *monogram.*

356. *Vase. Three-handled shouldered baluster form; running aquamarine, cobalt-blue, and purple-brown semi-matte glaze. Ht. 8¾ in. Marked* LCT *conjoined monogram,* 7.

357. *Vase. Inverted-baluster form; bubbly clear glaze with green, aquamarine, and cobalt-blue running areas over all. Ht. 15 in. Marked* LCT *conjoined monogram.*

358. *Goblet. Elongated ovoid cup on ribbed inverted-trumpet foot; clear, blue-gray, and white exterior glaze on cup with pale ochre and brown to black on foot, clear and brown interior glaze on cup and clear on foot. Ht. 9¼ in. Marked* LCT *conjoined monogram,* P1241 L. C. Tiffany-Favrile *Pottery.*

Pieces Reflecting an Influence of the Middle and Far East

359. *Vase. Ball-knop form; over-all golden-brown glaze with dark-brown trailings encircling stippled frieze with lions and highly stylized floral motifs. Ht. 6½ in. Marked* LCT *conjoined monogram,* 7.

360. *Vase. Inverted-baluster form; variegated silver-blue, gray-brown, ochre, and green glaze over all. Ht. 9½ in. Marked* LCT *conjoined monogram,* 7 P1085 L. C. Tiffany-Favrile *Pottery.*

361. *Vase. Oriental gourd form; mottled grass-green glaze over all; molded decoration of slightly swirling parallel ribs. Ht. 5 in. Marked* LCT *conjoined monogram,* 7.

362. *Vase. Oriental gourd form; variegated running green, yellow-green, and brown high glaze over all. Ht. 5¼ in. Marked* LCT *conjoined monogram,* 7 P825.

363. *Covered jar. Elongated incurved bucket form; mushroom-shape lid; variegated yellow-green glaze over all; molded branch-and-leaf decoration. Ht. over all, 9 in. Marked* LCT *conjoined monogram,* P15 LCT.

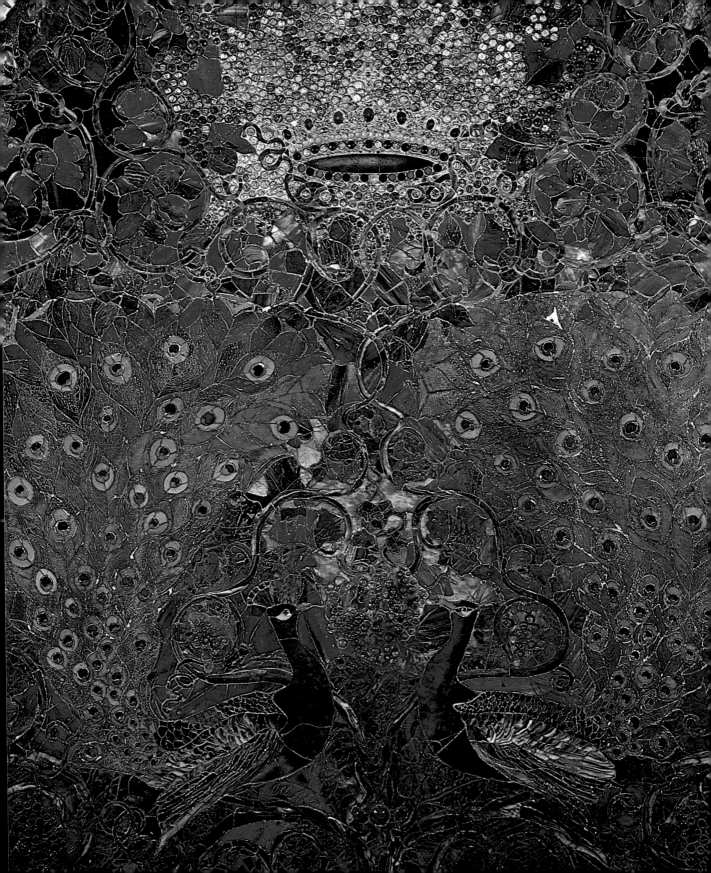

Peacock Reredos. Glass Mosaic on Plaster, from the World's Columbian Exposition Chapel, 1892 (#365)

*L*ouis Tiffany had a special feeling for the Chapel he designed for the World's Columbian Exposition in Chicago in 1893, and with good reason. The million and a half visitors who came to wonder at its brilliant windows and rich mosaics included critics and connoisseurs from all over the world, and by the time the exposition had closed Tiffany enjoyed an enviable international reputation.

The Romanesque-Byzantine treatment of its furnishings and mosaics was acclaimed as more creative and more American than the stately classicism of the exposition's famous "White City." Critics said the same thing of Louis Sullivan's "Golden Door" in the Transportation Building.

The Chapel was, in fact, a proving ground for many of the creative ideas stirring in Tiffany's busy mind. The beads and large garnets in the Peacock mosaic gave the niche a brilliance not found in the smooth surfaces of the mosaics of the time. They also anticipated the found objects which are so admired in the work of some of our modern masters. The altar candlesticks described by contemporary critics as a gold set with jewels, and which really are gilded lead set with quartz pebbles and glass chips, bring to mind the jewelry Tiffany made after 1900. This also is true of the door to the tabernacle with its mother-of-pearl, amber, and jade inserts. The electrolier was a hint of the imaginative use he would soon make of the electric light bulb. The leaded glass cover on the baptismal font was the antecedent of the leaded lampshades. The mosaics of mother-of-pearl, quartz pebbles, and glass in the altar front are forerunners of the miniature mosaic of precious and semiprecious stones in the "Peacock Necklace." The windows are filled with prototypes of the experimental glass his Corona glasshouse would soon turn out in vast quantities.

World's Columbian Exposition Chapel, Lectern and Altar (#366, 371)

When he was working on the Chapel, Tiffany's spirits were high. He was 44 years old and his home was blessed with children and happiness. His paintings in oil and watercolor had won him a place among America's leading painters (both watercolors and oils were destined to hang in the Fine Arts Building of the Exposition). As an interior decorator he had done countless American mansions, including Mark Twain's home in Hartford, Connecticut, and the public rooms of the White House.

And, perhaps best of all, since he was designing the Chapel for exhibition purposes, he was working for his favorite client — himself. Tiffany never liked having to please someone else. The Chapel reflects Tiffany at his happiest and best. He often referred to it, and rightly so, as "some of my finest work." That critics found it new, and above all, throughly American, pleased him very much. His affection for it was such that he wished to be buried from it, but that was not to be.

Chapel Font and Altar (#366, 370)

When the Exposition closed, Tiffany took the Chapel (the windows, mosaics, and furnishings) to New York and exhibited them in his studios. It was Celia Whipple Wallace, Chicago's famous "Diamond Queen," who had them installed in the crypt of New York's Cathedral of St. John the Divine as a memorial to her son. Since the original design of the cathedral was a form of Romanesque, Tiffany's Chapel fit in quite well, and services were held in it for many years. Ralph Adams Cram, when appointed architect for the cathedral, changed its style to Gothic and had Tiffany's Chapel boarded up.

In 1916, after years of neglect so tragic that the mosaics almost fell off the walls, Tiffany took the Chapel to Laurelton Hall, his country place in Oyster Bay, Long Island, and installed it in its own building near the mansion. He also designed the present cross as a replacement for the original which had somehow disappeared. The Chapel was included in his gifts to his Foundation.

*In 1946, the Trustees of the Louis Comfort Tiffany
Foundation gave the windows and furnishings to institutions which had little
interest in them, but left the mosaics in the abandoned building at Laurelton
Hall. When Jeannette and I learned the door was standing open and vandals
and scavengers were at work, we purchased the mosaics and contracted to have
them carefully cut up, packed, and shipped to Winter Park. The contractor cut
them carefully, but then tossed the pieces into the truck without any packing at
all. The trucking company, seeing an opportunity to reduce overhead, piled
household furniture on top of the mosaics, and a truck tire on top of the
furniture. What arrived in Winter Park was a discouraging sight.*

*Later, one of the colleges very kindly gave the windows in
their care to the Charles Hosmer Morse Foundation, but the institution that held
the altar and other furnishings asked a prohibitive price for them. Years later, on
learning the altar was being damaged by vandals, we purchased all the
furnishings.*

*Only a part of the mosaics is shown here. The concentric
arches that once rose over the Peacock Niche are in storage, as is a major part
of the electrolier.*

*The "Lily Window" is the original, without the angel which
once stood in its central part. Tiffany removed the angel himself.*

World's Columbian Exposition Chapel

364. *Chapel Door and Surround as installed at Laurelton Hall, ca. 1916. Oak and Iron 77 x 50 in. with surround 96 x 65½ in.; unsigned. Heavy oak adorned with pierced and overlaid wrought iron hinges and cross. A curved inscription of the front reads:* Knock and it shall be opened unto thee.

365. *Peacock Reredos, ca. 1892. Glass mosaic on plaster 90 x 72 in. Unsigned. From the World's Columbian Exposition Chapel. The design portrays the Vine, symbolizing the Sacrament of the Eucharist and the Peacocks which are symbolic of immortality.*

366. *Altar, with Retables and Tabernacle, ca. 1892. Marble, glass mosaic, glass jewels, abalone shell and semiprecious stones 39 x 94 x 50 in. Unsigned; from the World's Columbian Exposition Chapel. The Carrara marble mensa rests on a white glass mosaic frontal, consisting of approximately 150,000 tessarae; and decorated with the Apocalyptic emblems of the four Evangelists. The retables are also of Carrara marble with gold mosaic risers and an inscription from the sixth chapter of the Gospel according to St. John. Dividing the retables is a low rectangular tabernacle, whose door consists of a brass frame set with gilded lead came filigree and semiprecious stones.*

367. *Altar cross from the Chapel as installed at Laurelton Hall, ca. 1916. Unsigned. Brass, Favrile glass, mother-of-pearl; glass buttons and beads and gilded lead cames; Ht. 24 in.*

368.-369. *Four altar candlesticks, ca. 1892. Unsigned; from the World's Columbian Exposition Chapel. Gilded lead cames, woven brass, semiprecious stones and quartz pebbles; Ht. 36 in. All are of uniform size and shape but each varies in its material make-up.*

370. *Baptismal font, ca. 1892. Marble, blown glass, leaded glass, and glass mosaic; 63 x 42 in. Unsigned; from the World's Columbian Exposition Chapel. The spherical form of the font and its cover rests on seven marble and glass tesserae columns atop a two-tiered platform of marble and glass mosaic. The font is adorned with blown and pressed glass jewels, while the domed cover is silver backed glass leaded together in the manner of a lampshade.*

371. *Lectern, ca. 1892. Marble and glass mosaic. Ht. 54 in. Unsigned; from the World's Columbian Exposition Chapel. Of basic design, the lectern supported by three mosaic columns, rests on a mosaic frontal decorated with a circumscribed cross and sacred emblems.*

372. *Lectern candlestick, ca. 1892. Marble with glass and ceramic mosaic; Ht. 60 in. Unsigned; from the World's Columbian Exposition Chapel. One of a pair used on either side of the lectern.*

373. *Fragments of the electrolier, ca. 1892. Gilded metal and glass. Unsigned; from the World's Columbian Exposition Chapel. The electrolier was originally in the form of a Latin cross and was embellished with blown glass spheres, turtleback tiles and leaded glass panels. Tiffany cleverly integrated electrical lighting and was awarded a medal for harmonizing technology and aesthetic beauty.*

*T*he Art Work of Louis C. Tiffany *was written anonymously by Charles de Kay and published by Doubleday, Page and Company in 1914 for Tiffany's personal use. Of the 502 copies, 492 were on heavy rice paper and 10 on vellum. The cover on the latter was designed by Tiffany. The writing was supervised by Tiffany and is, therefore, a reliable record of what he thought about his own work and art in general. Its illustrations include the "Peacock Necklace," the "Entombment" and "Medallion" windows, and the Columbian Exposition Chapel.*

The vellum copy in this exhibition (No. 374) is autographed "No. 1 — To Mr. and Mrs. Charles L Tiffany, my dear son and daughter, Merry Xmas 1914." The copy in the blue paper binding (No. 375) is Tiffany's own copy.

The stenciled velvet is marked "Tiffany Fabric" on the selvage.

374. *The Art Work of Louis C. Tiffany. Copy No. 1 written anonymously by Charles de Kay. A Christmas gift from Louis C. Tiffany to his son and daughter-in-law (1914).*

375. *The Art Work of Louis C. Tiffany. Tiffany's personal copy.*

The Personal Mementos

The little chair (No. 380) was carried behind Tiffany in his later years as he walked around to inspect the windows, lamps, and other things being made at the Tiffany Studios. As time went on, he became a little unsteady on his feet. But his mind remained keen and his determination to maintain high standards never waned. He would scan a window with his bright blue eyes, punch out a piece of glass that did not suit him, select a new piece, have it put in the window, and move on. If and when he tired, he would sit right down without ever making certain the chair was there, and it always was. The chair may seem a little small, but considering his 5 ft. 6 in. height, it was big enough.

The handkerchief is carefully embroidered with "Louis Comfort Tiffany." The mahlstick (used by a painter to steady the hand) is the one he used all his life.

Personal Effects of Louis C. Tiffany

376. *Cufflinks in the form of books. Ivory and gold. Inscribed with L.C.T. monogram.*

377. *Handkerchief. Embroidered with* Louis C. Tiffany *(signature facsimile).*

378. *Mahlstick. Wood and brass. Used by Louis Tiffany when he painted.*

379. *Cardcase. Leather. Embossed;* Louis C. Tiffany.

380. *Chair from the Tiffany Studios. Wood and rush. This chair was carried behind Tiffany on his inspection rounds.*

Some of Tiffany's Awards

Tiffany was awarded 54 medals at the World's Columbian Exposition. In 1900, he was made Chevalier of the French Legion of Honor for his exhibit in the Paris International Exposition. This kind of recognition continued through the years before World War I. In the 1920s, the clean line and unadorned surface of the Bauhaus supplanted the floral elegance of Art Nouveau in public favor and Tiffany was passe. By 1930, he was forgotten or ignored.

The 28 medals and 12 award certificates (nos. 381-420) in this exhibit are handsome themselves, and they also tell of Tiffany's stature and fame.

The award from Eagleswood for "proficiency in drawing," given to Tiffany in 1864 when he was 16 years old, was the first. Eagleswood was a military academy. He had little freedom and a lot of discipline; he was homesick; his letters were corrected by one of the teachers; he was not good at spelling. When he received his diploma he announced to his father that enough was enough, that he would not attend college. Within a few months he was aboard the "Scotia," the fastest motor sailing ship afloat, on his way to Europe to travel, see the windows in the great cathedrals, sketch, and paint.

The diploma itself is drawn with pencil in the style of Tiffany's early drawings, and it is very likely that he made it himself.